4

AN ILLUSTRATED HISTORY OF
SEAPLANES & FLYING BOATS

AN ILLUSTRATED HISTORY OF
SEAPLANES &
FLYING BOATS

MAURICE ALLWARD

DORSET PRESS
New York

This edition published by Dorset Press,
a division of Marboro Books Corporation,
by arrangement with Moorland Publishing Co. Ltd
Ashbourne, Derbyshire, England
1988 Dorset Press

ISBN 0-88029-286-5

Printed in the United States of America
M 9 8 7 6 5

CONTENTS

ILLUSTRATIONS

6

1 SEAPLANE PIONEERS

It was a typical spring day at the little harbour of La Mède near Marseilles on the south coast of France. In the gently frothing Mediterranean a man in a dark suit and trilby hat sat on what appeared to be a length of two-barred farm fencing, gazing intently first at the weather and then at the calm surface of the water. Suddenly, with an abrupt roar the 'fence' started to move. Faster and faster still until, incredibly, it rose from the surface amid a flurry of spray and started to fly through the air. Few of the watchers on the shore realised that they were witnessing history in the making, with the world's first flight of a seaplane, on 28th March, 1910.

*   *   *

For centuries mankind has dreamed of flying machines that could travel through the air like birds. Many attempts must have been made that were not written down for posterity or, if they were, these records have not withstood the ravages of time. Some of the early records that have survived include references to 'boats' able to travel through the air, but the shape was almost certainly chosen because it had proved efficient for carrying passengers across the oceans, rather than because the 'flying boats' were intended to operate from water.

One such 'flying boat' is the one portrayed in a book published in 1670 by the Jesuit Father Francesco de Lana Terzi. De Lana's aerial ship comprised a boat-shaped body supported by four globes of thin copper, which were to be emptied of air. Thus lightened, they would rise, lifting the boat and its passengers with them. De Lana did not appreciate that such spheres would

9

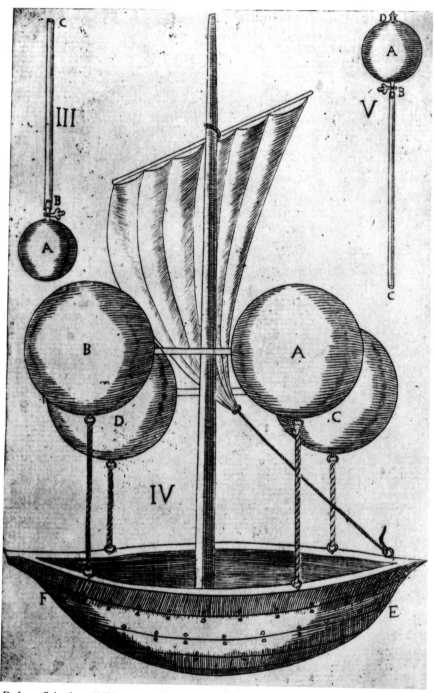

De Lana flying boat (1670)

immediately collapse under the pressure of the atmosphere. Nevertheless, he deserves credit for one of the first scientific approaches to the problem of flight, and paved the way for the first hot-air balloons and airships of two centuries later.

Sir George Cayley's famous boy and coachman-carrying gliders of the 1850s were actually built with boat-like fuselages.

In the late 19th century the idea of flying ships also seized the imagination of novelists. One such author was Frank Reade who, just before the turn of the century, produced a magazine of *'Invention, Travel and Adventure'*, the colourful covers of which often featured remarkably imaginative flying boats. These were big ocean-going vessels, equipped with multi-blade rotors to enable them to rise vertically from the sea and to hover over trouble spots, with air propellers for horizontal flight, so that they could travel over land at will.

The first serious design for an aircraft intended to take-off from and alight on water, however, was the amphibious two-seat monoplane designed by the French pioneer Bénaud, in 1874. In addition to its dual purpose retractable undercarriage, the prophetic design incorporated counter-rotating propellers, dihedral angle on the wings, a vertical fixed fin to which the rudder was hinged, an enclosed cockpit, a single control column operating the elevators and rudder, a compass, and a barometer for use as an altimeter. For its time this was a remarkable aircraft indeed.

A machine which, although it failed to fly, deserves a mention in this review of early attempts to fly from water, is the Wilhelm Kress twin-hulled tandem tri-plane built in Austria in 1901. This was the world's first powered marine aircraft. It was being tested and began to lift from the water when Kress saw an obstruction ahead, slackened speed, and tried to turn. The aircraft capsized and was wrecked. Later, Octave Chanute, the American pioneer, in a letter to Wilbur Wright commented that the aircraft possessed some excellent points in construction, and that it may well have flown if a lighter engine could have been obtained.

An aeroplane intended to operate over water if not actually from it, and one which very nearly flew before the Wright Brothers' aircraft, was the Langley "Aerodrome". This aircraft, a full-size replica of a successful powered model, was to be launched from a catapult on top of a houseboat on the river Potomac. Surprisingly, not only was it not fitted with a hull or floats, so that it could alight safely at the end of its flight on the water, but also no real provision was made for it to come down on land either. This omission is, however, only of academic interest as on the two occasions that the "Aerodrome" was launched in 1903, problems with the catapult gear caused it to crash during take-off.

11

Two years later, Gabriel Voisin, brother pioneer of Charles Voisin, produced a glider on floats that did work. This was built for Ernest Archdeacon, an aviation enthusiast, and consisted of parts of two giant 'Hargrave' boxkites mounted on two long canoe-like floats. When towed behind a motor boat on the river Seine, the glider actually lifted off the water, but it contributed little to the development of 'seaplanes'.

Even less successful was the float-glider produced by Voisin in conjunction with another famous pioneer, Louis Bleriot. This proved to be unstable and, after leaving the surface, side-slipped and crashed, nearly drowning Voisin, who wisely decided to abandon the Bleriot design.

Bleriot, however, dry and undeterred, continued the theme and designed his beautiful Bleriot III in 1906. In addition to the then still novel floats, the most unusual feature of the aircraft was that the tips of the biplane wings met to form a continuous ellipsoidal member. The tips of the large biplane tailplane also met in a similar manner. Such a design was quite impractical and the strange craft never flew.

The credit for making the first powered aircraft actually capable of taking off from and alighting properly on water, goes to another French pioneer, Henri Fabre, who made the historic flight of 28th March 1910, described at the beginning of the chapter. The term 'flying fence' is, perhaps, a little unkind, but it is certainly an apt description of Fabre's unusual *Hydravion,* the allusion being completed by the pilot's 'saddle' in the middle of the top 'rail'.

The strange craft appeared to fly 'backwards', due to the location of its twin-horizontal surfaces at the front, the single main wing being at the other end, behind the pilot. The top front surface acted as an elevator to provide a degree of pitch control, and lateral control was from four pedals which, through wires, warped the tips of the wing to act as ailerons. Operation of the rudder, which extended above and below the wing, was by an unusual tiller-like control which was also linked to the elevator. Even the wing construction was unusual; the main spar, a novel but structurally-efficient lattice-girder, was not enclosed within the surface but above it, acting as a support from which the wing ribs were suspended.

The wings were covered with canvas, stretched over the ribs and attached to each rib end by a sprung hook. By releasing the hooks, the canvas could be reefed up to the main spar like the sails of a boat. Some people considered the *Hydravion* more a boat than an aircraft. It was, in fact, once considered as an entry for a motor-boat race at Monte Carlo, rigged so that it could not rise completely clear of the water. Hearing this, a competitor said that he was thinking of carrying a gun in case the "*long-legged monstrosity*" looked like hopping over him!

12

THE ALDINE ROMANCE of INVENTION, TRAVEL, & ADVENTURE LIBRARY.

JULES VERNE OUTDONE !!!]

FRANK READE'S LATEST AIR WONDER the "KITE"

OR, SIX WEEKS' FLIGHT OVER THE ANDES

Far below lay the plain of Central Mexico. Frank and his comrades had not been so far above the sea level before.

No. 27]   [1d.
London: ALDINE PUBLISHING COMPANY.

Frank Reade flying boat

Impression of Benoist flying boats over St. Petersburgh, Florida (1914)

This description is also not entirely undeserved, for the three floats were carried on long spindly leg-like struts, one at the nose and two at the rear. The floats were made of plywood and were relatively flexible to help absorb the shocks of taxi-ing and landing. The front float was steerable for manoeuvring on the water. The floats had a flat bottom and a curved upper surface, the intention being that they should provide a lifting force both on the water and in the air.

The engine, a 37 kw (50 hp) Gnome rotary, was mounted at the extreme rear, aft of the wing. It spun round at about one thousand revolutions a minute and ran at two speeds — full and stop. With such crude engine control and the unusual configuration, Henri Fabre, who had never flown before, even as a passenger, deserves great credit for his achievement.

Curtiss flying boat, used for early auto pilot trials,

After several flights, including one of 6km (3.75 miles), the aircraft was seriously damaged while landing. It was rebuilt and extensively modified, but on the second flight in its new form it landed too close inshore, in the surf, and was again damaged. Fabre gave up the floatplane development and concentrated instead on the design and manufacture of floats. He did this well, supplying for example, all the floats used by the winning seaplanes in the Monaco Concours of 1913. It is, perhaps, for his float developments that Fabre should be honoured, rather than for his *Hydravion*, which was an aerodynamic freak.

Waterplane developments in the United States, although late, form a particularly important part in this branch of aviation. The American aviator-designer Glenn Curtiss had won a prize in 1910 of ten thousand dollars by flying from Albany to New York. The route, along the Hudson river, provided some anxious moments for the Curtiss *Albany Flyer,* a landplane.

Knowing the ease of mind that the ability to alight safely on water would

Sopwith Tabloid (1914) Schneider Trophy winner

have given him, Curtiss thought he had a simple solution to the problem of producing a waterplane. He merely took the wheels off one of his aircraft and mounted it on a canoe. Needless to say this hasty 'marriage' of two incompatible forms of transport did not work. Curtiss tried the same trick again, this time installing floats on his *June Bug,* which had won the *Scientific American* magazine's prize for the first public flight in the United States of more than a kilometre. Unfortunately, the engine was incapable of lifting the added weight. At this time also Curtiss, along with his contemporaries, did not fully appreciate the tendency of simple 'flat-bottomed' floats to 'stick' to the water as speed was increased.

Curtiss tried again, this time attaching a light, specially-designed, toboggan-like pontoon under the centre of a new aircraft. In this *'hydro aeroplane'* Curtiss succeeded in taking off, on 26th January 1911, to make the first such flight in America. Encouraged, Curtiss developed an improved pontoon, larger and more streamlined, and with this new *'hydroaeroplane'* attracted considerable interest by using it to pay a courtesy visit to the cruiser USS *Pennsylvania* moored in San Diego Bay. Alighting on the water, he was hoisted aboard the warship, and after a pleasant chat, was lowered back into the water and flew home. The trip so impressed officials that the Navy shortly after placed an order for its first floatplane.

Curtiss continued improving his waterplanes. One of his most important developments was the introduction of a 'step', or break, in the bottom surface of the pontoons. This reduced the suction of the water, which had kept his early aircraft, and those of many of his contemporaries, firmly glued to the water.

In January 1912 Curtiss carried things a stage further by replacing the pontoon of one of his *hydroaeroplanes* with a boat-like hull, in which the pilot could sit, instead of being perched on the lower wing. It was not a particularly aesthetic machine, and its engine developed only 45 kw (60 hp) driving two pusher propellers through a rather alarming system of gears and chains. It was, however, the world's first flying boat, and developments of it were purchased by wealthy sportsmen, and the US Army and Navy.

The successes of Curtiss encouraged and influenced other aviators both in the United States and overseas. One result of the encouragement was the formation of the Burgess Company, of Marblehead, Massachusetts. This Company started in business by producing Curtiss-type aircraft equipped with skid undercarriages. One interesting design of the Company was a hydroplane, powered by two engines driving four propellers, produced to win a prize of fifteen thousand dollars offered in 1912 for a twin-engined amphibian that could fly on one engine. Test flown in May, the aircraft proved that it could sustain flight on one engine, although it did not win the prize money, this being withdrawn by the sponsor as there were no other contestants.

In Britain, the Curtiss floatplanes and flying boats rekindled the interest of Mr Wakefield of Blackpool. Worried by the damage often sustained by the frail aircraft of those days through heavy landings on rough ground, Mr Wakefield had previously reasoned in 1909 that the solution was an aircraft able to rise from and alight on water. Not only did the self-levelling property of water remove the bumps, a splash into water seemed safer than a crash on land. At that time, however, his idea was ridiculed. This is understandable up to a point, as it was an achievement making an aeroplane fly at all in those days, without the complication and weight of floats or hulls.

Encouraged by Curtiss, however, Mr Wakefield returned to his idea, formed the Lakes Flying Company at Windermere, and commissioned A.V. Roe to build him a single-float seaplane based on the Curtiss biplane. This aircraft, named the *Water Hen* just missed being the first British seaplane, because, while it was being built, Cmdr. O. Schwann, R.N., fitted floats to an Avro biplane which was flown by S.V. Sippé in March 1912. But Wakefield's seaplane was the first entirely successful British waterplane, well justifying his faith in this type of aeroplane. The *Water Hen,* in fact, was flown almost daily without mishap throughout 1912, a remarkable achievement for those days.

Less successful, but technically innovative, was the Burney monoplane,

A.V. Roe floatplane (1912)

built by the British and Colonial (Bristol) Aeroplane Company and fitted with a 'Hydroped' water-under-carriage designed by Lt. Denniston Burney, inventor of the Navy mine-sweeping paravane. Designed to be attached to the hulls of flying boats, the 'Hydroped' consisted of three stalky legs, to which were mounted a series of hydrofoils and a water-propeller. The idea was that for take-off the pilot would start the engine and engage the water propeller only. As the aircraft moved forward and began to gain speed, the 'Hydroped' would begin to lift the hull clear of the water by 'stepping up' from one hydrofoil to the next. When he reached high speed and the bottom step, the pilot was supposed to engage the flying propeller and take off.

A prototype of the 'Hydroped' was made and when towed behind a destroyer took off like a kite but then immediately went out of control and crashed into the water.

Also of technical interest was a remarkable twin-hulled *Waterplane* flying boat built in 1913 by James Radley and E.C. Gordon England, and which had the added distinction of being the world's first three-engined aircraft. The three engines 37 kw (50 hp) Gnomes, were arranged in a row, like three discs on a single spindle, and drove a single propeller through chains. It was an odd arrangement, but gave the *Waterplane* a high degree of inherent safety as, if one engine failed, the flying boat could maintain height on the other two.

The reason for the twin-hulled layout was that Radley and England wanted to accommodate six passengers in comfort and did not believe that this could be achieved in the fuselage of a landplane. Each hull consisted of a large and rather fragile flat-bottomed float, containing three seats arranged clover-leaf pattern behind a small deck. The pilot sat in the front seat of the right hand hull, with two passengers behind him, and three more in the other hull.

The *Waterplane* was test flown initially as a landplane, with a simple wheeled undercarriage attached to each hull. It flew so well that England removed the wheels, after which he gave many demonstration flights from his base at Brighton. Unfortunately, alighting after one flight, England diverted his attention towards the other float to talk to the passengers, and so failed to see a marker-buoy, which ripped a large hole in the bottom of one of the hulls and the craft sank. The *Waterplane* was salvaged and rebuilt, with a single 112 kw (150 hp) Sunbeam engine instead of the three Gnomes, and the original hulls replaced by more robust ones of clinker construction, but it never flew again.

A more significant development in Britain was the famous *Bat Boat*, designed by T.O.M. Sopwith. Outstanding features of the *Bat Boat* was its beautifully finished, hand-sewn mahogany hull built by Sam Saunders, a boat building craftsman of Cowes. The *Bat Boat* was Europe's first successful flying boat and the world's first successful amphibian.

A *Bat Boat* was used in a series of pioneer bombing experiments by Sub.Lt. J.L. Travers and Lt. Bigsworth. During these Travers sat beside Bigsworth the pilot, with a bag of potatoes on his knees. On reaching a pre-selected field, Travers dropped the potatoes overboard one at a time, carefully noting the speed and height of the *Bat Boat* and the speed and direction of the wind at the moment he dropped each potato. On the ground Navy ratings observed the fall of each potato and marked its point of impact with a flag. As experience was gained, the potatoes were superseded first by specially shaped darts and then by 'bombs'. In this manner Travers gained valuable data on the behaviour of objects dropped from aircraft, which formed the basis of the bomb-aiming techniques developed by the Royal Naval Air Service. A *Bat Boat* was exhibited at the 1913 Aero Show at Olympia. It so attracted the interest of the First Lord of the Admiralty, Mr Winston Churchill, that he issued instructions that it be purchased for the Royal Naval Air Service.

In France, the influence of Curtiss caused the designer Denhaut to fit a pontoon-hull to his Donnet-Lévêque pusher biplane. In this instance the combination was both handsome and efficient, and the aircraft participated in many of the early air meetings and air races in Europe.

An event of considerable interest occured on 1st January 1914. On that day the St Petersburg-Tampa Airboat Line began a passenger service between the two towns. The aircraft used were Benoist flying boats, and the

32 km (20 miles) flight saved passengers a motor car drive of nearly twice that distance, while the time saved was even greater; twenty minutes by air against two hours by motor car. The little flying boats carried only the pilot and one passenger, who paid five dollars for a flight, yet they made two round trips a day for four months before the world's first 'scheduled' airline also become the first, but not the last, to go out of business. The time was not yet for passenger-carrying, airliner-type flying boats.

While this marine aviation was underway, the clouds of war had been darkening the European horizon. This fact, and the offer by Lord Northcliffe, of the London *Daily Mail* of a prize of fifty thousand pounds for the first transatlantic flight, attracted the attention of Rodman Wanamaker, heir to the U.S. Wanamaker Department Stores fortune.

Accordingly, in 1914, Wanamaker commissioned Curtiss to build him a large flying boat capable of crossing this formidable ocean. To help him in this ambitious project, Curtiss engaged the services of an enthusiastic British Naval pilot, Lt. John C Porte. The aircraft, named the *America*, had a wing span of 22.5m (74ft) and was the biggest aircraft ever built in the United States.

Wanamaker hoped that the crossing of the Atlantic by his *America*, a joint British-US venture, would, in addition to winning the prize money, demonstrate the importance of aviation to all the nations of the Earth, celebrate a hundred years of peace between Britain and the United States — and last but not least — prove once and for all that it was time for the entire world to disarm. Such a long-ranging flying-boat, Wanamaker hoped, would render war futile.

A study of the *America* gives the impression that with minor development it might well have achieved the distinction of being the first aircraft to cross the Atlantic, but whether its subsidiary anti-war aim would have been realised is open to doubt.

In the event, the *America* did not have the chance of proving itself. For, just as the flying boat completed its initial trials, Britain and France became engaged in bitter war with Germany. World War One had started.

2 FLYING BOATS AT WAR—WORLD WAR I

The military potential of aircraft had been a spur to their early development. Military trials had been held, notably the first *Concours Militaire* at Reims in 1911, and those in Britain and Italy during which torpedoes were dropped from aircraft. However when hostilities broke in August 1914, none of the great powers had a clear idea of either the purpose or use of aircraft as a weapon of war. This was especially true of those specialised aircraft designed to operate from water, the seaplanes and flying boats.

A few visionaries had advocated that aircraft could be used for reconnaissance. In fact, they had already been used for this purpose, when, on 23rd October 1911, a Bleriot XI of the Italian Army participated in the Italo-Turkish War by reconnoitring the Turkish positions near Azizia. Among the pre-war visionaries in Britain was a small group of Admiralty officers who allowed and encouraged in 1911 the training of the first four Royal Navy officers as pilots, and who in 1912 purchased a two-seater FBA biplane, which thus became the first flying boat to enter Royal Naval service.

Another British pre-war visionary, also of the Admiralty, was Winston Churchill, who as First Lord in October 1913, had recommended the following types of aircraft for duties with the Royal Navy; *"an overseas fighting seaplane to operate from a ship or base, a scouting seaplane to work with the fleet at sea, and a home service fighting aircraft to repel enemy aircraft ..."* Churchill's enthusiasm for seaplanes had resulted in an early purchase of a Sopwith *Bat Boat* for the RNAS.

One result of this official enthusiasm was that when the British Home

21

Fleet was reviewed at Spithead in July 1914 by HM King George V, the flypast of aeroplanes included seventeen Short and Farman seaplanes.

Water-borne aircraft had received their baptism of fire before the start of World War I. The Austro-Hungarian forces used Viennese-built Lohner flying boats extensively in the Adriatic area during the Balkan War of 1913, being the first combatants to introduce waterbased aircraft. During this conflict the Austrian Navy assigned its first seaplanes, three French Donnet-Lévêques, to the naval base at Kotor on the Balkan coast, later re-inforcing them with American Curtiss and German Etrich aircraft.

The Lohner was a two-seat, reconnaissance, patrol and bombing biplane, with a central hull-fuselage and the engine was mounted between the wings driving a pusher propeller. The fuselage, designed with particular care, was made of wood and in spite of a rather big cross-section, was a good compromise between the conflicting requirements of seaworthiness and aerodynamics. The tail unit was mounted distinctively above the 'stern'. The first production aircraft, known as Model E, was powered by a 63 kw (85 hp) Hiero engine, and forty were built during 1914 and 1915. The most widely used version was the much improved Model L, powered by a more powerful 105 kw (140 hp) Austro-Daimler or Hiero-Warchalowski engine. The aircraft had a crew of two, and could carry up to 50 kg (110lb) of bombs or 200 kg (440lb) of anti-submarine depth charges on racks attached to the sides of the hull. Defensive armament was usually a single Schwarzlose machine-gun, firing forward. A searchlight was carried as standard equipment and some of the aircraft were equipped with radio transmitters.

A total of 108 Lohner Ls were built in Austria. In addition, 140 Lohners were built in Italy by Macchi following the capture of one of the Austrian machines. The first 'copy' aircraft was completed in the record time of 34 days. The performance of the Italian-built aircraft was somewhat superior to that of the Austrian originals because of the more powerful engines installed. One of the Italian 'boats' was equipped with a 23mm cannon for anti-submarine duties.

The Austrian Lohners were used on many attacks against Italian targets along the Adriatic coast. Most of the missions involved night bombing operations, and were carried out by groups of six or seven aircraft. Cities bombed included Venice, Ancora, Rimini, Ravenna and Brindisi. On the night of 1st June 1916, a Lohner engaged and shot down a Caproni Ca.3 bomber near Trieste after it had been picked up by Austrian searchlights.

Later on that month Lohners inflicted heavy damage on the Italian destroyer *Zeffiro* and two torpedo-boat destroyers, the *Fuciliere* and *Alpino*. On 9th September 1917, they made a night attack on an airship repair hanger and destroyed it and the airship M.8. A similar attack on 26th September resulted in the destruction of the airship M.13.

The most notable Lohner operation, however, was undoubtedly the engagement on 15th September 1916 when two of the flying boats attacked and sank the French submarine *Foucault* in the Adriatic. After the attack, the Lohners landed in the sea and took survivors of the French crew prisoner. The submarine was an old steam-powered vessel of little military value, but its destruction by a flying boat is an important milestone in the history of military aviation.

The Armistice of 1918 deprived Austria of a sea border, and she had no use for seaplanes. The Austro-Italian flying boats, however, formed the nucleus of the Italian Adriatic reconnaissance-bombing force, and were the basis of a long and successful programme in the development of Italian naval aviation.

*　　*　　*

In spite of the early developments in Britain, when war broke out with Germany, the aircraft available to the services were of little practical military value for other than reconnaissance work. In particular, Britain's Royal Naval Air Service flying boat force consisted of a single Donnet Lévêque, the prototype White and Thomson single-engined Curtiss-type flying boat and one or two Sopwith *Bat Boats*. Many officers soon began to wish they had more, as experience showed that the more numerous but less robust floatplanes readily broke up in choppy seas.

At the outbreak of war John Porte, then helping Curtiss in the development of the *America* transatlantic flying boat, immediately left the United States to rejoin the British Navy.

Once he was back in the service, Porte recommended the purchase of two Curtiss *Americas* H-4 flying boats, and upon their arrival in Britain these were sent to Felixstowe, where they were tested by Porte himself. He quickly discovered that their take-off performance was poor through bad hull design. The hulls embodied only a single step, with the result that the water resistance was so great before the critical speed for hydroplaning that it was often impossible to take-off. To achieve a wing angle of attack of 15 degrees required for maximum lift, the nose had to be raised until the tail dragged in the water, as there was insufficient change of angle between the main hull and the tail to keep the latter clear. The 'boats' also pounded alarmingly when taxi-ing in choppy seas.

One RNAS pilot who flew the H-4 flying boats later described them as *"comic machines, ... with two comic engines giving, when they*

Italian built Lohner

functioned, 180 horse-power; and comic control, being nose-heavy with engines on and tail heavy in a glide".

Porte asked Curtiss to develop a larger boat, with more powerful engines, a longer range, and able to carry a bigger pay-load. Curtiss responded quickly and by the late summer of 1916 improved flying boats, powered by two 119 kw (160 hp) Curtiss engines, began to arrive in Britain. Designated H-12, these were referred to as *'Large Americas'*, to distinguish them from the earlier *'Small Americas'*.

In spite of their more powerful engines, the first thing Porte did was to take them out and replace them with 205 kw (275 hp) Rolls-Royce Eagles. It was with this engine that they became one of the most useful anti-submarine, anti-Zeppelin and reconnaissance aircraft operated by the RNAS.

To overcome the shortcomings of the original H-4 *Small Americas,* Porte was given the task of developing a more seaworthy hull. The first form involved relatively minor changes to the basic *"America"* hull and were only moderately successful. For his fifth hull, however, Porte abandoned the boatlike monocoque hull in favour of a slab-sided "fuselage" built upon four longerons, with normal vertical and horizontal spacing members and diagonal bracing. The V-shaped planing bottom, of cedar and mahogany, embodied three steps and was constructed as a secondary structure, which was secured to the bottom of the "fuselage". The tail was angled up in order to provide ample clearance when taking off and alighting. To this new hull Porte attached the wings and engine of an H-4 *Small America.*

Thus was born the *Porte 1,* or F-1, the first of a range of Felixstowe flying boats, which revolutionised flying boat design and which gave Britain a lead in this type of aircraft which she maintained for nearly a quarter of a century. Heartened by his success, Porte decided to produce an improved version of the *Large America* using the same principles. The result was the Porte II, or F-2 craft, from which was developed the superb F-2A, F-3 and F-5 flying boats which rendered outstanding service with the RNAS and RAF for many years.

Unfortunately, all this development work took time and it was not until 1917 that sufficient large flying boats were available to play a major part against German U-boats and Zeppelins, by which time Britain had suffered almost crippling shipping losses. But, once the big boats went into action, they proved their effectiveness against submarines.

During the First World War the North Sea was dominated by the battleship navies of Britain and Germany. In this theatre, the object of the Royal Navy was to entice the smaller German fleet into battle so that it could be destroyed, while the objective of the German Navy was to protect the U-boat routes to the Atlantic, and so whittle down the overall British supremacy piecemeal over a period of time. These tactics compelled Britain to keep the North Sea Fleet perpetually at the ready in case the Germans attempted a break out. The effectiveness of German battleship broadsides was demonstrated during bombardments of Hartlepool, Whitby, Scarborough, Great Yarmouth and Felixstowe.

In executing these bombardments the German Navy was ably assisted by reconnaissance carried out by Zeppelins. Thus, in addition to anti-U-boat patrols, the 'Felixstowe' flying boats were also used for anti-Zeppelin duties.

An encounter between these two fundamentally different forms of air vessel was an event to remember, as indicated by Lt.Robinson, pilot of an F-2A. His official account is recorded in the Report of Naval Operations for May 1918 as follows:

"May 30th — Killingholme — Seaplane No 4291 (the term seaplane was

Sopwith Bat Boat

often used for flying boats as well as floatplanes). *Pilots Lieut Robinson and Ensign Hodges (USN). Whilst on patrol, at 11.20, when in position 325 p, sighted a Zeppelin on the port bow about 7 miles distant, flying approximately 10,000 ft. Course altered to attack and enemy engaged for 10 minutes at a range of 4000 ft ... "*

Zeppelins could outclimb F-2As, and as soon as the flying boat was sighted, the nose of the huge airship was lifted and the craft began to gain altitude. To reduce the disparity in climb performance F-2As on anti-Zeppelin patrols carried a reduced crew of four and no bombs, partly to save weight and partly so more petrol could be carried. However, on this occasion the 'lightened' F-2A's struggle to gain height was unsuccessful.

There were five gun positions on the F-2A; two Lewis guns in the nose on a Scarff ring, a gun over the second pilot firing forward, a dorsal gun aft of the wings, and a flank gun on each side of the hull, in line with the dorsal gun. When not in use the flank gun ports were covered by a sliding hatch. When required, these were slid rearward on the outside of the hull when the guns, which were on a hinged arm, could be swung over. The crew used whichever position was the most convenient, moving from one to the other.

During this particular attack Lt. Robinson was in the 1st pilot's seat, on the starboard side and Ensign Hodges was manning the nose gun. At a distance of 1,200 m (4,000 ft) the flying boat crew could not positively identify the Zeppelin beyond the fact that it was one of the latest vessels in the new super class. Also, at that extreme range, it was not possible to assess what damage, if any, was inflicted. However, the attack was not a complete waste of effort, as in order to evade the F-2A, the Zeppelin jettisoned so much of her useful load, water, bombs and fuel, that she aborted the mission and returned to base.

However, it was on anti-submarine duties that the flying boats were most active and proved most effective as far as the overall effect on the war was concerned.

During the last eighteen months of the war, the Felixstowe-modified Curtiss and the F-series of flying boats were involved in many events of gallantry and achievement. Most of those involve operations in the vicinity of the North Hinder light ship, for it was here that the famous 'spider web' flying boat patrol pattern was centred.

By intercepting wireless messages, the British authorities knew that large numbers of U-boats were passing through this area in the Spring of 1917, on their way to selected areas around the English coast. To conserve the electric batteries which powered the U-boats when they were submerged, the German vessels generally travelled on the surface. On the surface, however, they were a perfect target for a flying boat provided they could be detected amid the vast expanses of the North Sea.

To locate them a pattern of search was evolved, known as the 'spider web', which enabled four aircraft to search the whole area in less than five hours. The web comprised an octagonal figure, 100 km (60 miles) across, with eight radiating arms 50 km (30 miles) in length, with three sets of circumferential lines, joining the arms at distances of 16, 32 and 50 km (10, 20 and 30 miles) from the centre.

Eight sections were thus provided for patrol, covering about 10,000 sq km (4,000 square miles) right across the path of the U-boats, which were also in danger of being spotted if they were within 16 km (ten miles) of the outside of the web.

At their average cruising speed it took a U-boat 10 hours to cross the web, whereas a single flying boat could search a quarter of the whole area in five hours.

The first Spider Web patrol was flown on 13th April, 1917 and the operation soon proved its worth. Although only five boats were available,

27 patrols were made in the first 18 days, during which eight U-boats were sighted, three of which were bombed.

On 20th May Flt.Sub Lt. C.R. Morrish and his crew of a *Large America* scored the first positive success of the Felixstowe boats by sinking U-boat UC.36 near the North Hinder lightship. Sighting the submarine at a distance of about 8 km (five miles), the flying boat initially flew over it to ensure that it was an enemy vessel, and then went into the attack just as the craft started to crash dive. The bombs hit the submarine squarely in front of the conning tower and it sank almost immediately.

At the time this was thought to be the first confirmed sinking of a submarine by an aircraft and has been recorded as such in many early books. As described earlier, however, this particular first was achieved by the two Austrian Lohners which sank the French submarine *Foucault*.

To counter the Spider Web patrols, the Germans despatched fighter seaplanes to shoot down the flying boats. To counter the seaplanes, the flying boats themselves took up the offensive and, armed with a full complement of guns, went out hunting aircraft as well as U-boats. There ensued a bitter period of attack and counter-attack that lasted many months.

In addition to direct attacks on the flying boats, the Germans also turned their attention to their bases. Two heavy raids were made on Felixstowe in July 1917, in which one flying boat was destroyed, another severely damaged, and twenty-four naval ratings killed or badly wounded. The offensive efficiency of the base was not impaired, however, for in the week following the second attack, Felixstowe flying boats sank two more U-boats.

The flying boats also turned their attention to Zeppelins. Like U-boats, these often inadvertently revealed their position by transmitting wireless signals; and in April 1917 the British authorities decided that as soon as a Zeppelin was detected within 240 km (150 miles) of the English coast, one or more flying boats would be despatched to hunt for it.

One such mission took place on 14th May 1917, when a *Large America,* commanded by Flt Lt C.J. Galpin, armed with three machine-guns and bombs, and carrying extra fuel for the long flight, set out from Yarmouth to hunt a Zeppelin reported to be near the Terschelling light vessel.

After a short while, radio contact with Yarmouth was suspended in case the flying boat gave its position away to the Zeppelin! Half an hour later, at 4.48 am, the Zeppelin was sighted, dead ahead and about 24 km (15 miles) away. It was on patrol, cruising slowly at 900 km (3,000 ft), and quite unaware of the fate rapidly approaching out of the clouds and fog.

Aboard the flying boat, now flying at 111 km/h (60 knots) and some

900 m (3,000 ft) higher than the Zeppelin, the crew took up action stations. Galpin manned the forward guns, with Flt.Sub-Lt. R. Leckie at the controls. When he was within 0.8 km (half-a-mile) of the Zeppelin, Leckie pushed down the nose of the flying boat to gain speed. This distance between the two aircraft closed rapidly, and Galpin managed to get in a good burst of fire from a range of only 180 m (200 yards) before both his guns jammed, and Leckie banked steeply away while they were cleared.

Another attack was not necessary, for as the flying boat turned, its crew saw a sinister red light glowing within the envelope of the Zeppelin. Within seconds the glow became a mass of flames, and the stricken airship dropped tail first towards the sea. Only 45 seconds after the initial attack the blazing skeleton of L.22 splashed into the water, leaving only a layer of glowing ash on the surface and a column of black smoke to mark its funeral pyre.

One month later a *Large America* from Felixstowe, piloted by Flt.Sub-Lt. B.D.Hobbs attacked and destroyed Zeppelin L.43 off Vlieland.

After these two losses the German Zeppelin crews became more wary. They patrolled at higher altitudes, and kept a sharp look-out for the British flying boats, knowing that as they could outclimb them under normal conditions; all they had to avoid was a surprise attack.

To overcome this tactic, the Admiralty introduced mixed patrols of one *Large America* accompanied by a de Havilland DH.4 high-performance day bomber, especially modified for long-range anti-Zeppelin duties. The method of operation was for the flying boat to carry out a feint attack on any Zeppelin sighted. This manoeuvre would almost certainly cause the airship to concentrate on climbing unsuspectingly to get out of range — and in so doing provide an easy target for the DH.4 cruising at a higher altitude.

The first of the new mixed patrols was flown on 5th September 1917, and very nearly achieved success. Sighting Zeppelin L.44 cruising at a height of 3,000m (10,000ft) Sq.Cmdr. V. Nicholl flew his flying boat straight toward the big airship. As expected, the Zeppelin started to climb. For half an hour the two craft exchanged fire, while Flt.Lt. A.H.H. Gilligan in the DH.4 tried in vain to outclimb the Zeppelin so that he could make his attack. Unfortunately, the engine of the DH.4 proved troublesome and he had to break off the action at 4,300 m (14,000 ft).

The sequal to this engagement was that on the way back to base, the engine of the DH.4 seized up completely and the aircraft ditched in the sea some 80 km (50 miles) off Yarmouth. Exercising considerable skill Nicholl put his flying boat down alongside the stricken DH.4 and, despite a heavy sea, managed to pick up Gilligan and his observer just before their aircraft sank. However, it was not possible to take off again with the two extra airmen aboard, and Gilligan started to taxi home. Unfortunately, his fuel gave out after a time, and the flying boat and its crew drifted helplessly for three days and nights, before being sighted by *HMS Halcyon*. The rescue came just in time as the crew of the flying boat had reached the limits of their endurance, and they probably would not have survived so long but for Nicholl's leadership, for which he was awarded the DSO.

*   *   *

Flying boats also played their part in areas other than the North Sea. Flying boats based in the Scilly Isles, off Cornwall, helped to escort and protect Allied convoys in the dangerous waters of the English Channel. Another aircraft, based at Dunkirk in North France, with an escort of Sopwith Camel fighters, attacked and sank U-boat UC.72 on 22nd September 1917. In May 1918 one of Porte's modified F.2A flying boats from Killingholme air station attacked Zeppelin L.62 and after a long running fight sent it down in flames. Other flying boats based at Donisbristle, Inverness, Scapa Flow, Plymouth, Falmouth, Pembroke Dock and Blackpool played their part in keeping Britain's vitally important sea-lanes open.

Between the grimmer episodes of the anti-Zeppelin and anti-U-boat war there were the inevitable touches of humour. Felixstowe, under the command of John Porte, was a happy station. Among its strength were many 'characters' who refused to let shortages of equipment or even bombs get in the way of what they considered was their 'private war' over the sea.

So keen were they to fly, that in order to permit operations in fog, pilots are said to have devised a way of landing in such conditions. Apparently, they carried a long stick, which was fitted, before alighting, in a vertical socket outside the hull so that the lower end projected several feet below the bottom of the hull. The socket was coupled to the control column, so that when the end of the stick dragged on the water it pulled the control column back and the flying boat levelled out and alighted safely. High spirits were not a monopoly of Flexistowe. A young student pilot at Killingholme, reprimanded for not flying according to the book, went out and demonstrated his feelings by looping an F-flying boat over the station.

The launching and beaching of floatplanes presented many difficulties and the officers at Yarmouth set about to solve the problem. The result was the *'GRW wheel float attachment'*, the initials being those of the surnames of the three inventors. The device was simple but effective. It consisted of no more than a pair of wheels which could be fixed to each main float, and which could be released either when the aircraft was afloat or airborne; a single sprung wheel was attached to the tail float. Thus equipped a

30

floatplane could simply taxi straight into the sea and the wheels released when it was afloat. For beaching, the float plane was brought close inshore and the wheels attached, when it could taxi out of the water and straight up the beach unaided. Without the *'GRW'* wheels, a cumbersome trolley and large handling party was required.

The performance of some of the early floatplanes left much to be desired, as this recollection of a Short 20 by an officer who served at Great Yarmouth indicates:

"The general routine of patrols was a submarine patrol on the Short some time during the forenoon on those very rare occasions when the seaplane would get off. It was a two-seater machine that would only carry the pilot, and was noted for its capacity to sling oil. The pilot flew with two 7 kg (16 lb) Hale bombs on his lap, bomb frames being far too scarce in those days to fit an ordinary seaplane, besides the extra weight stopped her 'getting off'. On one occasion it was known to have reached the prodigious altitude of 300m (1,000 feet); the pilot, a very harmless, innocent 'quirk', hardly fledged, straight from Chingford, having struggled with the machine for hours, came home so full of life that he told everyone, even the Commanding Officer, of his experience. 'What the hell do you mean by doing a submarine patrol at that height for? You would never see a submarine from 300m (1,000 feet), even if it was there!' and that was all the thanks he got from his Commanding Officer".

Inventive innovation was not confined to the men actually in the front line. The *Large America* and F-2A flying boats, with their ability to fly for

Short 225 seaplane (1916)

more than six hours with a useful load of bombs, and their comparative safety for long-range over-water missions, were sometimes sent as far north as Terschelling on reconnaissance and anti-Zeppelin patrols.

In the autumn of 1916, however, the Admiralty had plans to extend their radius of action even further — to Germany itself, in order to assist an intended bombing offensive against German North Sea ports.

The plans involved the use of special lighters, barge-like vessels, each able to carry a *Large America*, and strong enough to be towed at speeds of up to 55 km/h (30 knots) behind a destroyer. Loading of the aircraft on to the lighters was to be accomplished by flooding tanks in the latter so that it submerged, when the flying boat could be floated over it and then raised clear of the surface.

Orders were placed for four lighters in January 1917, and within eight months, the first had successfully completed initial tests at Calshot and on the Solent, followed by trials in the North Sea. In calm weather, the lighter was towed at speeds of up to 59 km/h (32 knots). So promising were the trials that production orders were placed for fifty lighters.

The first operational trial was conducted on 19th March, 1918. For this, three flying boats from the original test batch of four were used for a sortie over the Heligoland Bight area. At 5.30 am on that day, three destroyers, each towing a lighter with its aircraft, and supporting craft, arrived off the German coast. Ninety minutes later all three flying boats were airborne and heading north-east towards the reconnaissance area. The appearance of the large aircraft in their home waters naturally surprised the Germans. However they quickly recovered and sent up two seaplanes to intercept them. During the ensuing battle, one seaplane was shot down, after which the flying boats completed their mission and returned safely to base.

So useful was the intelligence information gained, that the Admiralty ordered a repeat operation only two days later. This mission also proved highly successful, the flying boats spotting a large force of minesweepers at work clearing an area to the north of Ameland and Terschelling. Armed with this knowledge, the Royal Navy was able to counter all the German hard work by laying a new minefield on 2nd April.

Lighter-borne operations continued until the end of the war in November 1918, the F-2A and *America* flying boats surveilling German activities around Heligoland, while their counterparts from Yarmouth reconnoitered the Terschelling minefields. Often the flying boats met fierce opposition from apposing German seaplanes, and a number were lost. The information gained, however, was considered to more than justify the cost and losses involved.

The British authorities had realised from the beginning that the lighter-borne operation had its limitations. For one thing, good weather was absolutely essential. The long term answer was obviously a bigger flying boat, with a very much longer range and able to carry a really heavy bomb load.

John Porte had, in fact, produced such an aircraft in 1916. It had a wing span of 37.79m (124 feet) and weighed about 8⅔ tons fully loaded. It was easily the biggest aircraft built in Britain up to that time which makes its name, the *Porte Baby*, something of a paradox. However, its performance was inferior to that of the Porte II(F2) boats and so it was not developed or put into production.

It has earned its niche in flying boat lore, however, by pioneering the 'composite aircraft' idea, rejuvenated successfully twenty years later in the Short-Mayo flying boat. In the case of the *Porte Baby*, a tiny Bristol Bullet fighter was mounted on its top wing. The idea was that the flying boat would carry the small high-speed fighter far out over the North Sea and then launch it in search of Zeppelins, thus overcoming the problem of the fighter's short range. During trials the Bullet, piloted by Ft.Lt Day, was actually launched successfully from the flying boat in mid air. However, the scheme was not considered so practical as the *Large America* — DH.4 mixed patrol already described, and was not developed further.

The *'Baby'* was not Porte's biggest boat, for in 1917 he completed a giant aircraft with three wings and five engines. Known as the *Felixstowe Ferry,* this weighed 14,968 kg (33,000 lb) and could carry 24 people and fuel for seven hours; ten years were to pass before any other British boat equalled its weight lifting capacity. It was successfully flown by Porte, but failed while taking off in April 1919 at the hands of another pilot due, apparently, to incorrect loading which moved the centre of gravity too far aft.

In spite of their comparative limitations and fragility, floatplanes were used extensively by Britain as well as Germany. The potential of this type of seaplane had been demonstrated in 1911, when Captain Guidoni took off in an 80 hp Farman carrying a small 160 kg (352 lb) torpedo and successfully dropped it whilst airborne. In Britain 1913 saw the first floatplane flight with a 35 cm (14 in) 408 kg (900 lb) torpedo and also the first order for a floatplane specially designed to carry this formidable weapon.

In August 1914 three Short *'Folder'* seaplanes were modified to carry torpedoes. Three early seaplane carriers were rapidly produced by the hurried conversion of the cross-Channel steamers, *Empress, Engadine* and *Riviera.* The idea was that these ships would take torpedo-carrying aircraft far out in the North Sea. In the event the Short aircraft were never used to drop torpedoes, primarily because operational requirements kept the carrier vessels employed on other duties.

Three Short 119 kw (160 hp) Folder seaplanes went to Africa early in 1915 to assist the British Navy's attempts to cripple the German light cruiser *Konigsberg*, which was then lying in the Rufiji delta. The first air reconnaissance of the German warship had been made by a 67 kw (90 hp) Curtiss flying boat, originally the property of a Durban mining engineer. The Curtiss flying boat was wrecked and two Sopwith 807's, which arrived in February 1915, proved unsuitable. The three Short seaplanes arrived at Durban in March aboard the armed liner *Laconia*, and reached Niororo Island at the end of April. The aircraft made several reconnaissance flights to keep an eye on the situation and the *Konigsberg* was eventually put out of action by the British monitors *Mersey* and *Severn* on 11th July, 1915.

One of the most widely used floatplanes in the war was the Short 184 of 1915. This was a large span biplane, powered by a 167 kw (225 hp) Sunbeam engine. Officially designated the "Short Seaplane Admiralty Type 184" or Short 184, and known affectionately among RNAS personnel as the Short Two-Two-Five (after the horse-power of the engine) it was built in hundreds and used in all theatres of operations.

Its structure was typical of the period, the fuselage being a wire-braced wooden box-girder covered with fabric, and the wings, which could be folded, were also of fabric-covered wood. The main floats were large wooden pontoons, transversely connected by arched cross-members which contained the torpedo crutches.

On 21st May, 1915, the seaplane carrier *Ben-my-Chree*, a converted packet-boat, sailed from England for the Dardanelles, with three Short 184s and two Sopwith Schneider seaplanes on board. The unofficial intention of the commander was to torpedo two particular enemy vessels, the *Göeben* and the *Breslau*. The *Ben-my-Chree* arrived at Iero Bay, Mitylene, on 12th June, 1915, and two months later one of the Short 184s scored a direct hit with a torpedo on an enemy vessel. Even though he flew without an observer to save weight and carried fuel for only a 45 minute flight, the pilot, Flt.Cmdr C.H.K. Edmonds, was not able to climb any higher than 240m (800 ft). When within range of the vessel, a Turkish supply ship, Edwards glided down to within 4.5m (15 ft) of the water and released his torpedo at a range of 320m (350 yards) to score a direct hit amidships.

At the time this was thought to be the first time a ship had been sunk by an aerial torpedo, but it later transpired that the Turkish vessel had already been torpedoed and shelled four days earlier by a British submarine and was in fact beached in shallow water when attacked by the Short floatplane. The action, however, clearly demonstrated that it was possible to drop a torpedo from an aircraft and strike a selected target.

34

Felixstowe F 2B on patrol

Five days later, two of the Short 184s each sank an enemy vessel, one under most unusual circumstances. One Short 184 launched its torpedo at three steamships at anchor and hit the middle one. The pilot of the second Short, however, had engine trouble on the way to the target area and, in the words of the official report on the action *". . . was forced to descend in the Straights without reaching Ak Bashi Liman"*. He saw a steam tug on the Asiatic shore, taxied in, and torpedoed it whilst under rifle fire, and then taxied away towards Bulair. His engine developed a few more revolutions, so he managed to get off, and crossing Bulair at about 60 m (200 ft) reached the ship.

In that climate it required nearly new machines to lift the torpedo, and unfortunately lack of such new machines prevented the attacks from being repeated.

Otherwise, by seriously interrupting the Turk's maritime communications (about one third of his supplies) the torpedo seaplanes might have largely affected the campaign.

The engines of the Short floatplanes were often so troublesome that when one came back from a patrol, its engine was immediately taken out and a

35

rebuilt motor installed. The removed engine was taken into the on-board workshops, taken completely to pieces and rebuilt with new valves.

After these early successes, however, no other torpedo attacks were made by the Short 184s in any theatre of war, and the type gained the greater part of its reputation as a patrol seaplane and bomber.

In European waters, carrier-borne Shorts of HMS *Riviera* and *Engadine* made several sorties against the North German coast during the winter of 1915-16, but the missions were hampered by frequent engine trouble.

A Short 184, No. 8359, gained the distinction of being the only aircraft of any type to participate in a major naval battle during the war. On 31st May 1916, the British Grand Fleet put to sea to engage the German fleet steaming off Jutland. HMS *Engadine* sailed from Rosyth with the Battle Cruiser Fleet.

At 2.20 pm the light cruiser *Galatea* signalled 'Enemy in sight', and the *Engadine* was ordered to send a seaplane to scout the area. Soon Short No.8359 was airborne and during a 40-minute flight sent back four messages before a petrol pipe broke and compelled it to come down in the water. The pilot repaired the fracture with a piece of rubber lining from his life-jacket but, upon reporting his readiness to continue, was told to return to the *Engadine*. By one of those wartime strokes of misfortune, the reconnaissance did not assist the British fleet, as the *Engadine* was unable to pass the messages on to Sir David Beatty commanding the Grand Fleet.

Short 184s were used as night bombers to aid the RNAS Fifth Wing's campaign in late 1916. Other Short 184s served in Mesopotamia in February 1916 where, operating from the Tigris at Ora they helped to drop supplies to the besieged town of Kut-al-Imara.

Significant numbers of the floatplanes operated in the Mediterranean, in addition to those of the East Indies and Egypt Seaplane Squadron. The seaplane base at Otranto was originally equipped with six 184s transferred from Dundee air station and in the following month a torpedo seaplane school equipped with 184s was established in Malta. Nearly 400 Short floatplanes, most of them 184s, were in service with the Royal Air Force when the war ended in November 1918.

Four years of grim war had shown that both floatplanes and flying boats were able to undertake a wide variety of tasks under difficult conditions, tasks which could not have been performed by landbased aircraft. In particular, the seaplanes had demonstrated well their unique advantage of not requiring prepared lasting strips from which to operate. It was this advantage that caused seaplanes to be used for a number of pioneering long range flights in the coming years of peace.

3 FLIGHTS OF ADVENTURE

Four years of war had a dramatic effect on aviation. In Britain alone the industry grew from a few scattered visionary craftsmen and even fewer scattered factories, into a vast complex industry, employing 350,000 people and producing aeroplanes at the rate of nearly 30,000 a year. Similar growth took place in France, Germany, the United States and, to a lesser extent, in Russia.

With the return of peace many pilots and manufacturers assumed that aircraft would soon be busy carrying passengers and goods between the capitals and business centres of the world. But the expected boom in civil aviation did not take place. In fact, it did not really come for nearly another half century, until the mid nineteen-fifties, when the combination of big aircraft and package tours, resulting in a drastic reduction in fares, at a time of increased prosperity, brought air travel within reach of millions of ordinary people for the first time. Nevertheless, at the end of the War, the air routes of the world were there to be conquered and exploited, and there was no shortage of men willing to stake their fortunes or even their lives on a gamble to be first in the field.

One obvious important air route of the future was the Atlantic Ocean, dividing as it did the Old and New Worlds. In May 1919 the great ocean was indeed conquered, appropriately by a flying boat of the U.S. Navy, a Curtiss NC-4. This was one of three aircraft that departed from Trepassey Bay, Newfoundland, on 16th May 1919. Two were forced down into the ocean, but the survivor flew on via the Azores to Lisbon and Plymouth, having taken 12 days for the complete journey. This flight demonstrated the inherent safety of the flying boat for overwater operations. The crew of one

Supermarine Channel

downed aircraft was rescued by a British ship, and the other crew was picked up by a US destroyer.

In Britain, serious official thought had been given to the possibility of establishing civil air services as early as 1917, while the War was still raging. In that year a committee had been set up to *'deliberate on questions affecting the commercial use of aircraft in the period immediately following the war.'* The committee concluded that there would indeed be a market for the carriage of mail and perishable foodstuffs, but that the main source of revenue would come from passengers. Reviewing the work of the committee, the British aviation magazine *The Aeroplane* commented that the flying boat should prove particularly attractive for civil use, because *'by its use one great difficulty of aviation is at once eliminated, and that is the provision of landing grounds. As aircraft grow larger the question of landing space will become more and more prominent. But over the sea there is little difficulty. The flying boat can be increased in size to any limit commensurate with efficiency, and there will always be room to alight without laying waste land possessing other and greater uses.'*

When one contemplates the vast expanses of concrete now covering some of the best farming land in countries all over the world, one can but wonder at the wisdom of the turn aviation took away from waterborne aircraft after World War Two, even though the reasons for the turn are understood.

In 1919, as if to prove *The Aeroplane* correct, an F-5 was despatched from Felixstowe on a 3,942 km (2,450 miles) tour of Scandinavia to demonstrate the commercial possibilities of flying boats. The F-5 achieved its objective admirably, for the craft suffered no hold-ups or mishap of any kind during the twenty-seven days it was away from its base. This was a remarkable achievement for that time, particularly as the flying boat was the very first F-5 built.

In those days a flight did not have to be a long one for it to be adventurous. In 1919 Hubert Scott Paine's Supermarine Company began a flying boat service between Southampton and Le Havre. The aircraft used, known appropriately as the Channel type, was developed from a small military flying boat built by Supermarine during the war. Powered by a 119 kw (160 hp) Beardmore engine, they carried three passengers in addition to the pilot. The low power meant that take-off was sometimes a lengthy process, causing one passenger to comment sarcastically that, on short journeys, it might be less trouble to taxi all the way!

To overcome the power problem, the Channels were re-engined with a 180 kw (240 hp) Puma, and a redesigned front step fitted to the hull to ensure cleaner running. The changes must have made the little flying boats satisfactory, as during the next few years they were used in Bermuda,

Douglas World Cruiser *Chicago*, over Asia

British Guiana, Chile, Japan, New Zealand, Norway, Sweden and Trinidad.

The use of the Channels in New Zealand, for carrying mail in the Auckland area, was typical of the jobs done by these little boats. Lack of adequate surface transport combined with an abundance of waterways and inland lakes, made this an ideal region for flying boat operation. Indicative of the improvements in time was the linking of Dargaville with Auckland in eighty minutes, compared with seventeen hours by train and steamer.

Channel flying boats were also used for an early air survey, involving air photography, of part of the Orinoco Delta for an oil company. No other type of aircraft could have been used as the crocodile and mosquito infested area was so flooded and swampy that there was not even enough dry land upon which to set up a base camp. The aircrews and surveyors had to live in a cluster of huts built on barges. Unfortunately, in spite of the hard work by the ground crews and skilful flying by pilots, many of these pioneering companies were compelled to close down due to lack of support. Such a fate befell the cross-channel flying boat service.

In Britain, the Government was aware of the potential of civil aviation, and further proof was provided in 1920 when the Air Ministry organised a series of competitions to encourage the development of civil passenger-carrying aircraft. First prize of £10,000 in the Amphibian Class was won by a Vickers Viking, while a Supermarine three-seat Commercial Amphibian won the second prize.

The Viking achieved its niche in history, first by being built under licence in Canada, pioneering that country's home aircraft industry, and secondly by landing on the Thames and taxi-ing ashore at Parliament where it was inspected by the Members. Subsequently, the Viking was developed into the Vulture amphibian in which Sqdn.Ldr A.S.C. MacLaren and Flt.Lt. W.N. Plenderleith made a gallant effort to fly round the world in 1924. Starting at Calshot, the Vulture covered about 21,000 km (13,000 miles) reaching the Bering Sea, before the attempt had to be abandoned.

However, this historic 'first' was achieved by seaplanes that very year. The aircraft, four Douglas *World Cruisers,* designed especially for the flight, were named after American cities: *Boston, Chicago, New Orleans* and *Seattle.* They are often depicted with a wheeled undercarriage, but earn their inclusion in this review of waterborne aircraft because for most of the long flight they were fitted with floats. Powered by a 313 kw (420 hp) Liberty engine the 15.24 m (50 ft) span aircraft had a maximum cruising range of 2,655 km (1,650 miles) with floats, and 3,540 km (2,200 miles) with wheels. Although well-equipped depots were established all along the route, each aircraft carried a full set of tools considered sufficient for all envisaged

Douglas World Cruiser *Boston,* refuelling

maintenance operations during the long voyage. In this sophisticated age of electronics, hydraulics and advanced technology the tool kit makes fascinating reading: *"hammer, pliers, screwdriver, spanner and a torch."*

Fitted with floats, the four aircraft took off from Seattle on 6th April 1924 and headed for their first stop, Prince Rupert, 972 km (605 miles) distant. The route then continued via the Aleutian Islands, Japan, China, the Middle East, Europe, Britain, Iceland, Greenland and the U.S.A.

Only two aircraft, the *Chicago* and the *New Orleans* completed the flight. The *Seattle* scraped a float against a fog-hidden mountain top near Dutch Harbour, Alaska and crashed. Fortunately the crew, Frederick Martin and Alva Harvey were unhurt, although it took ten days of walking through the wilderness to cross the Alaskan Peninsular and find sanctuary at a small fishing village near Port Moeller on the Bering Sea. The *Boston* was forced down by engine trouble in the North Atlantic, skilful piloting bringing the little aircraft down safely on the crest of a swell. The crew of this aircraft, Leigh Wade and Henry Ogden, were rescued by the US Navy cruiser *USS Richmond*, but the *World Cruiser* sank while being towed to the Faeroe Islands for repairs. The *Chicago*, with Lowell Smith and Leslie Arnold, and the *New Orleans*, with Erik Nelson and John Harding, finally returned to Seattle on 28th September 1924. The 44,342 km (27,553 mile) flight had taken 175 days, of which 371 hours were flying time.

*　　*　　*

Three years later a waterborne aircraft was used for another great voyage of adventure, a 32,000 km (20,000 mile) survey flight round Africa by Sir Alan Cobham.

This particular flight was the culmination of a series of flights made by Sir Alan to demonstrate how air transport could link together more closely the widely scattered countries of the British Empire. Many of the early flights, involving landplanes, required prepared landing grounds. For the first flight round the Dark Continent, however, Sir Alan had chosen an aircraft completely independent of such grounds, the prototype of the magnificent new Short Singapore I, the first of a new breed of all-metal flying boats.

During this remarkable flight, the only mooring facility provided at most of the pre-arranged stopping places was a simple buoy. If, as sometimes happened, this broke adrift, then the aircraft's own anchor was used.

Near disaster overtook the Singapore at the beginning of the flight when adverse winds required an emergency landing in St. Paul's Bay, Malta, at night and in a swell. When daylight came the flying boat was flown over to the nearby Royal Air Force base at Cala Frana, where a more sheltered anchorage was available. A safe landing was made, but as the Singapore was being towed to shelter, one of the notorious Mediterranean storms sprang up and a huge wave tore away the starboard wing tip float, causing the aircraft to lurch dangerously over to that side. The big aircraft was only saved from almost certain destruction by members of the crew who quickly clambered up the opposite wing to keep the aircraft on an even keel, despite big waves which broke continually over them. As soon as possible the crew members were replaced by 90 kg (200 lb) bags of sand.

Two days later, the weather calmed and the Singapore was towed towards the beach for repair. Before the craft could be beached, however, the storm broke out again with renewed force. It increased steadily in fury during the next two days, preventing repeated attempts to drag the damaged craft

44

Short Singapore 1, used by Sir Alan Cobham

ashore. Waves washed away the other wing float and the port wing sank into the sea while the craft began drifting towards a pile of rocks. Just when her complete destruction seemed inevitable, a huge wave lifted the crippled flying boat up and smashed it down on one of the slipways.

Royal Air Force personnel immediately dragged the Singapore clear of the shore line, but even then she was not safe. Big roller-waves began crashing over her hull. In the waves were huge rocks and, one by one, the tail surfaces were smashed away. Her complete loss was certain and in an attempt to salvage at least part of the aircraft, servicemen dragged her over a sea wall to comparative safety, in doing so smashing completely the damaged port wing.

When the gale subsided the Singapore looked a sorry sight. Yet the ground crew simply fitted a new port wing, new wing tip floats and tail surfaces to make the craft airworthy, and it then went on to complete the survey of Africa. The 'Malta-incident' is a tribute to the sturdiness and reliability of flying boats in general.

Sikorsky S-38 *Kauai* over an extinct volcano in Hawaii

Sikorsky S-38 *Ark* used for African safari

Floatplanes and flying boats were also used extensively to open up another great continent, South America. The inaugural flight of the then fledgling airline, Pan American Airways, was made by a Fairchild FC-2 floatplane, when it carried mail between Key West, Florida and the Cuban capital, Havana. The use of a floatplane was, however, accidental. It was planned to use a Fokker Trimotor, but on the day when the airline had contracted with the US Post Office to begin the mail service, 19th October, 1927, the Dutch aircraft had not been delivered. Frantic with worry officials of the airline stood at Key West not knowing what to do, when out of the blue there splashed down the little single-engined Fairchild floatplane. The pilot had merely stopped to refuel, but the Pan American manager, showing great initiative, asked him if he would carry the mail to Havana — for a small consideration, of course. The pilot, a cheerful Cy Caldwell, agreed, and the historic flight was made.

The important Florida-Cuba route was 'won' by a determined ex-Navy

Supermarine Air Yacht

bomber pilot named Juan Trippe, destined to create one of the world's greatest airlines. The mail contract had, in fact, already been awarded to another airline, but Trippe paid a personal visit to the Cuban dictator, Gerardo Machado, and obtained from him an exclusive flying permit, which meant that no other airline could land or take off from Cuba.

Although Trippe planned to use Fokker Trimotor landplanes for his Key West-to-Havana mail service, the then virgin Caribbean as a whole was ideally suited to waterborne aircraft. In fact, as early as 1919 a Navy surplus Curtiss F-5-L was used to operate passenger flights between Key West and Florida. For a while the service flourished — flying people out of 'dry' America (Prohibition was then in force) to Havana, where alcohol was not only plentiful but cheap.

Curtiss, however, did not pursue the development of flying boats after the war, and so Juan Trippe turned to a small firm known as the Sikorsky Aero Engineering Corporation. The president, Igor Sikorsky, a refugee from the Russian Revolution of 1917, had already established himself as a pioneer of multi-engined aircraft; during the war he had produced seventy of the world's first four-engined bombers.

In 1926 the Sikorsky company produced the S-36, a twin-engined amphibian. It was an unusual craft, the tail surfaces being mounted on two

Sopwith Schneider seaplane

distinctive booms extending aft of the wing. The boat-like hull, suspended from the wing on struts, accommodated eight passengers. The hull was 10.36 m (34 ft) long and the wing span 21.94m (72 ft). Only five S-36s were built, and of these only one went to Pan American. It was this single S-36 flying boat, however, which spearheaded the Pan American conquest of the Carribean. Even though it was slightly underpowered, it had a good performance, and, of course, it could alight on both land and water. As Andre Priester, Pan American's chief engineer commented, "*A seaplane carries its own airport on its bottom.*"

Encouraged by the technical success of the S-36, if not by its sales, Sikorsky produced a ten-seater development, the S-38, powered by two 300 kw (400 hp) Pratt and Whitney Wasp engines. Like its predecessor it was an ungainly-looking machine, described unkindly by one engineer as "*a collection of aeroplane parts flying in formation*". But, known affectionately to those who flew in it as the *'Ugly Duckling'* and the *'Flying Tadpole',* it was a most practical amphibian. It could take-off and climb on one engine, and its introduction helped both the commercial success of Sikorsky and the expansion of Pan American. Juan Trippe went about this

Supermarine S.6B

expansion with the vigour of a British 18th century privateer, causing as much woe among his opponents as did those sea-faring predecessors. In building his aviation empire, Trippe had a staunch ally in Walter F Brown, the U.S. Postmaster General, whose plans to provide an efficient air mail service to South America coincided with Trippe's ambitions. The chief weapon in this early expansion of Pan American, however, was the S-38.

Soon the little amphibian was making survey flights down both coasts of South America. Charles Lindbergh used the aircraft for many of his survey flights on behalf of Pan American. To gain publicity, two newsmen were taken on a tour of the airline's American routes. In 17 days they visited 20 Latin-American countries covering a distance of over 29,000 km, (18,000 miles) of the Pan American system. The trip took them over two great oceans, desert, jungle, high mountains and rolling plains . . . Pan American had expanded its 180 km (110 mile) Key West-to-Havana route twenty times in less than four years.

During the hectic planning of new routes and the business of revenue-earning flights, Pan American found time to make a number of mercy missions. One such flight resulted from the violent earthquake which devastated large parts of Managua in Nicaragua on 31st March, 1931. The damage cut all communications with the stricken city, in which large numbers of people had been killed or wounded. Hearing of the devastation, Pan American head office diverted an airborne S-38 to the area. The amphibian set down in Managua Bay and, with the help of its radio, aid was soon coming in from every direction.

*   *   *

While these long adventurous flights were being made, other much shorter, but equally exciting flights were also thrilling the world. These were the races for the bronze Trophy which had been presented by the French armaments manufacturer Jacques Schneider to the Aero Club de France in 1912. The object of the Trophy was to encourage the development of seaplanes which Schneider considered had been neglected in favour of landplanes. Any country winning the Trophy three times in succession could keep it in perpetuity.

Right from the first race in 1913, however, it was a contest of sheer speed rather than seaworthiness. This race, held at Monaco, was won by a Deperdussin monoplane, fitted with floats, at a speed of 74 km/h (46 mph) which at least showed that the seaplane had arrived. The second race in 1914 was won by another floatplane, a Sopwith biplane specially designed for the event. Britain had her second success in 1922 at Naples with the Supermarine Sea Lion II flying boat, the brainchild of a budding young designer, R.J. Mitchell. In 1923 the United States entered for the first time and won the Trophy with a Curtiss CR-3 seaplane at a speed of 285 km/h (177 mph).

The American victory emphasised the importance of reducing head resistance by design features such as streamlined cowling of engines and wing radiators, of metal propellers and low weight-to-power ratios plus, last but not least, the need for efficient organisation on the ground.

Public interest in the Schneider Trophy mounted and it grew into the outstanding aircraft contest in the world. The winning aircraft was taken to epitomise its country's aeronautical prowess. In 1925 America won for the second time, again with a Curtiss, at a speed of 374 km/h (233 mph) in the hands of a pilot whose name was soon to become world famous — James Doolittle. Britain entered two aircraft for this contest, a Supermarine S-4 monoplane racer designed by R.J. Mitchell, and a Gloster biplane. The S-4 crashed before the race and the Gloster aircraft was easily beaten, as was the Italian aircraft.

Undiscouraged, the Italian company *Aeronautica Macchi,* inspired by Mussolini, produced in six months a distinctive monoplane known as the M.39 designed around a new Fiat engine. This aircraft won the 1926 race, thus ousting the supremacy of the Curtiss biplanes. It is a good thing for Britain that the Italians did win; had the Americans done so it would have given them three victories in a row and permanent possession of the Trophy.

Before the S-4 crashed it had set a seaplane record of 364 km/h (226 mph). The merits of the design were thus obvious and Mitchell was asked to produce three new seaplanes for the 1927 contest based on the S-4. The result was the S-5, a low-wing, wire-braced monoplane, smaller than the S-4. For the 1927 contest, held at Venice, the Italians designed the beautiful M.52, which glistened with lacquered wings and french-polished ailerons.

One Supermarine S-5 came in first at a speed of 454 km/h (282 mph) and the other second. All the Italian aircraft were forced to retire, much to the bitter disappointment of many thousands of emotional national spectators.

To defend the Trophy in 1929, the British Air Ministry commissioned Supermarine to build two further seaplanes. The new aircraft, designated S-6, were the first of the Mitchell high-speed designs to be powered by a Rolls-Royce engine. The S-6 was the smallest possible airframe which could be built around the new liquid-cooled 1,200 kw (1,600 hp) Rolls-Royce R engine. A feature of technical ingenuity was the use of double-skin wing-surface radiators of light alloy.

An S-6 won the 1929 contest, held over the Solent, and later raised the world speed record to 576 km/h (358 mph). Britain had now won twice in a row and needed only one more victory to win the Trophy outright. The 1931 contest was thus of great significance and the Supermarine morale sank when, in a mean economy, the British Government decided it would not finance an entry. Disaster was averted only by the generous financial help from the rich and patriotic Lady Houston. Supermarine were unable to design a completely new aircraft, but Mitchell produced a series of refinements which were embodied in two aircraft known as S.6Bs.

These aircraft, representing the ultimate in aerodynamic refinement, won the 1931 contest with a speed of 547.31 km/h (340.08 mph). With this victory Britain gained permanent possession of the Schneider Trophy. Later that year the other S.6B was flown at 656 km/h (407 mph) to gain the World Air Speed Record for Great Britain, becoming in the process the first aircraft in the world to exceed 643 km/h (400 mph).

The experience gained during the development of the Supermarine S-4, S-5, S-6 and S-6B aircraft was used as the foundation for one of the best known landplanes of all time — the *Spitfire* fighter, which played such an important part in World War Two.

4 MILITARY DEVELOPMENTS

When World War One ended, the pace of military aviation development slowed. Known to many of the combatants as the *'Wars to end Wars'*, there was neither the resolve, need nor money for major military pursuits.

One seaplane which would have undoubtedly proved an unpleasant surprise to its enemy had the war continued was a remarkable little single-seat fighter flying boat called the *Baby* produced by Supermarine in February 1918. The world's first fighter flying boat, this was designed especially to counter the *Brandenburg* fighters used by Germany to patrol the North Sea. Extremely small, the *Baby* had a wing span of just over 9.14 m (30ft) and was powered by a 112 kw (150 hp) Hispano-Suiza engine driving a four-bladed pusher propeller. Its performance, including a maximum speed of 188 km/h (117 mph) and superb manoeuvrability, compared favourably with land-based fighters of the time.

The *Baby* did not go into production, but the design formed the basis of the *Sea King* and *Sea Lion* civil prototypes, and the famous *Walrus* amphibian of 1933. Designed for shipboard use and stressed for catapulting from warships, the 474 kw (635 hp) Pegasus-engined *Walrus* had an extremely rugged structure. The single-bay wing arrangement was intended to ease the rigging problems arising from the loads imposed during catapult operations. To reduce drag, the wheels retracted neatly into wells in the bottom wing. The pilot sat in an enclosed cockpit and there were gun positions in the bows and aft of the wings.

The *Walrus* became the standard Fleet 'spotter' on all catapult-equipped warships of the Royal Navy. It was used for artillery spotting, anti-submarine, convoy patrol and communications duties, the latter including, on occasion, service as the Admiral's Barge. It achieved its greatest fame, perhaps, during World War Two, when on air-sea rescue duties, it rescued many ditched aircrews. Carrying beer ashore to thirsty infantrymen was also a popular task.

Supermarine's skill at producing flying boats so impressed the Air Ministry that the company was asked to design a new aircraft to replace the ageing F-5 for coastal defence and Fleet co-operation. The result was the *Southampton*, the prototype of which was built, tested and delivered in the short space of seven-and-a-half months. Distinctive features of the *Southampton* were the adjustable cantilever tailplane with triple fins and rudders, the W-arrangement of the centre interplane wing struts and the unusual mountings of the two 350 kw (470 hp) Napier Lion engines.

A crew of five was carried, comprising two pilots in tandem open cockpits, a wireless operator/air gunner in a cabin amidships, a front gunner/bomb aimer in the bows, and a second gunner in a cockpit aft of the wings. Facilities for cooking, recreation and sleeping were provided in cabins in the spacious wooden hull.

The first post-war flying boat to enter Squadron Service with the Royal Air Force, the *Southampton* was ahead of any other flying boat in its class at the time, and had a normal range of 1,240 km (770 miles) a service ceiling of 4,270 m (14,000 ft) and a top speed of 173 km/h (108 mph). Its sea worthiness was ably demonstrated in September 1925, when four *Southamptons* made a 16,000 km (10,000 miles) cruise around the Irish Sea, much of it in bad weather.

This was followed by several famous long distance flights used by the Royal Air Force for training purposes. The first of these was an 11,300 km (7,000 miles) cruise during the summer of 1925 to Egypt and Cyprus and back to prove the independence of flying boats from prepared bases. On 14th October 1927 four *Southamptons* left Britain for a 43,000 km (27,000 mile) flight to Australia and Hong Kong. Within a few months the same four aircraft made another impressive long distance flight of some 30,000 km (19,000 miles) from Hong Kong to Nicobar and the Andamans. Later *Southamptons* were fitted with duralumin hulls and 373 kw (500 hp) Napier Lion VA engines, these being the major Royal Air Force type.

Another large flying boat to enter service with the Royal Air Force in the mid-twenties was the Blackburn *Iris* which, powered by three 504 kw (675 hp) Rolls-Royce Condor engines and with a wing span of 30 m (95 ft), was one of the biggest aircraft of that time. Like the *Southampton*, it had a crew of five, but the hull layout was quite different. The two pilots sat side-by-side in a large cockpit in the bow just aft of which was a single cockpit for the navigator. Gun positions were provided in front of the pilots, amidships

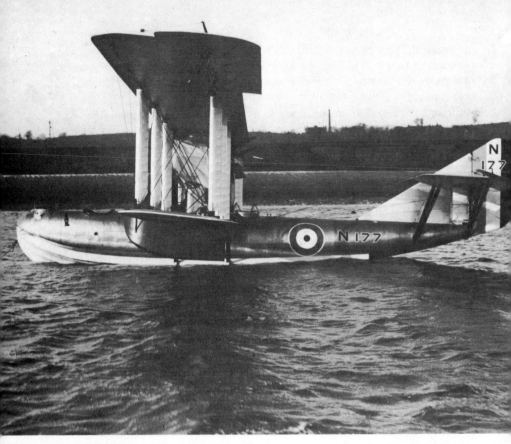

Short F.5 with metal hull

and aft of the wings. A distinctive feature of the wooden aircraft was the large biplane tail unit, mounted on the upswept stern of the hull.

In this period of general peace, *Iris* flying boats made many memorable flights. In 1927 one machine, fitted with a metal hull, and accompanied by three other flying boats, a *Valkyrie,* a *Southampton* and a *Singapore*, made a 15,100 km (9,400 mile) Baltic cruise. Acting as flagship, the *Iris* carried Sir Samuel Hoare, Britain's Secretary of State for Air. In 1928 another *Iris* made a 27,000 km (17,000 miles) tour to India and back. The next year *Iris* took part in the search for the submarine H-47, which sank in tragic circumstances in the Channel. In this year, 1929, an improved version, known as the *Iris III,* was developed. This embodied revised hull accommodation, with facilities for cooking, sleeping and repair work, to make the aircraft a self-contained unit.

Dominating the British military flying boats during this period, however, were those produced by Shorts, who developed a revolutionary method of construction. First indication of this new method appeared in 1920, when Shorts built their little *Silver Streak*, the first aeroplane in the world to have an all-metal, stressed-skin monocoque fuselage. Not only was this method of construction lighter and stronger than wood-and-fabric; it was more suitable for quick production. Another advantage was that the absence of internal bracing greatly increased the useful space inside a fuselage.

As far as flying-boats were concerned, a major advantage of this method of construction was that it overcame the serious problem whereby wooden hulls of the time significantly increased weight in service through soaking up water. It did not take the Air Ministry long to realise that metal hulls would solve many of the worst headaches of flying boat operations, especially in areas where shore facilities were minimal or non-existent.

To prove the idea, Shorts built an experimental duralumin stressed-skin hull to replace the wooden hull of an F-5, and the tiny *Cockle* single-seat monoplane flying boat also using duralumin. With this experience Shorts were given a contract to build an all-metal version of the *Cromarty,* built in 1921 as a replacement for the F-5, but which did not go into production.

The result was the superb Singapore prototype of 1926, which was used by Sir Alan Cobham for his famous survey flight round Africa. The *Singapore I* powered by two 485 kw (650 hp) Rolls-Royce Condor engines and with a wing span of 28.34 m (93 ft), was the first of the big all-metal flying boats.

Only one *Singapore I* was built, but it was followed in 1930 by the much improved *Singapore II*. Powered by four 392 kw (525 hp) Rolls-Royce Kestrels, this was the first Short flying boat to use the twin tandem engine layout, which doubled the power available without the drag of two extra nacelles. To reduce drag further a single-bay wing strut arrangement was adopted, and the hull was of fine streamline form.

In 1934 The *Singapore II* was followed by the *Singapore III*, last of Short's biplane flying boats. Powered by four improved Kestrel engines each developing 545 kw (730 hp), this variant had a crew of six, a maximum speed of 233 km/h (145 mph), a range of 1,600 km (1,000 miles) and a touch-down speed of 105 km/h (65 mph).

Duties of the *Singapore III* included special patrols from Malta in 1937 to protect British shipping during the Spanish Civil War. Spectacular incidents included the skilful landing on a small tree-surrounded lake in Kent, England, following the fracture of some tail support struts. The failure of

Supermarine Walrus

Blackburn Iris

the tail incidence gear in flight of another *Singapore III* over Iraq caused the aircraft to climb and dive alternately in an alarming manner until the fractured component responsible for the antics could be lashed with a spare cable from the rear gunner's cockpit.

The *Singapore III* was probably the best military flying boat in the world in its time. It flew majestically in both rough and calm weather over the blue seas of the Mediterranean and the Far East. A few remained on active service for a short period after the outbreak of World War Two, both in Britain and the Far East. In 1941 three *Singapores* comprised the sole air defence of Fiji!

*　　*　　*

Short Singapore II

The days of the biplane were clearly numbered, and a much improved successor to the *Singapore* had, fortunately, flown two years before the War started. This was the military counterpart to the civil Empire flying boats ordered by Imperial Airways and will be described in the next chapter.

Known as the *Sunderland I*, this was an all-metal monoplane flying boat powered by four 754 kw (1,010 hp) Bristol Pegasus radial engines. The distinctively deep hull was divided into two decks. The lower deck contained crew rest rooms, galley and a mooring compartment in the bows. The crew, consisting of two pilots, flight engineer, navigator and wireless operator were all accommodated in a large cabin at the forward end of the upper

63

deck. Aft of this cabin was the 'bomb bay', from which loaded racks, carrying up to 900 kg (2,000 lb) of bombs, were run out on rails through hinged panels in the side, to their dropping position under the wing. The prototype was armed with two power-operated gun turrets, the bow turret containing one .303 in machine-gun and the stern turret housing four machine-guns of the same calibre. To improve the defensive capability, two additional gunners' cockpits were soon introduced in port and starboard upper beam positions; these gunners had single, free-mounted machine-guns. When war broke out in September 1939, four *Sunderland* squadrons were operational.

Two years before the *Sunderland* appeared, Dornier in Germany produced the DO 18, one of a series of fine tandem-engined flying boats built by this company. Fast and reliable, the DO 18 set a long-distance seaplane record of 8,437 km (5,242 miles) in March 1938. In common with most German civil aircraft of the thirties, there was a military version, the DO 18K, with gun positions in the bows and in the wing between the engines. Another Dornier civil flying boat of which there was a military version was the three-engined DO 24.

Another energetic producer of seaplanes in Germany was Heinkel, who had supplied S.1 monoplane twin-float aircraft to the Swedish Air Force in the late twenties. When the new German Air Force was formed, Heinkel produced a long succession of float planes, including the He 59, a twin-engined biplane; the He 60, a smaller version of the He 59; the He 114, an odd-looking sesquiplane, and the He 115, a fast torpedo-carrying monoplane. One of the best spotter reconnaissance float planes produced during this period was the *Arado* Ar 196, a two-seat monoplane, which was carried on a number of German warships.

Although not successful, one of the interesting military floatplane developments of the late nineteen-twenties was the Parnall *Peto*. This was a very small floatplane, specially designed to operate from the Royal Navy submarine M2. Because of its intended use the *Peto* was constructed largely of stainless steel. The M2 was the last of three M-class submarine monitors with an armament of one 12-in gun and four 18-in torpedo tubes built during World War One. The gun was housed in a large turret and on the M2 the gun was removed and the turret adapted for use as a small hangar. The little *Peto* was launched from a catapult extending from the hangar. After completing its mission the floatplane set down alongside the submarine and was recovered by means of a crane fitted to the top of the hangar.

During trials the *Peto* was launched and recovered several times. The operation was popular with the pilots concerned, partly because of its novelty, and partly because they received both flying pay and submarine

Dornier Do 18

pay. However, the idea was not developed, as the *Peto* did not have the speed or ceiling performance considered desirable while the submarine, with its bulky hangar, was an unwieldy vessel to handle. The M.2 was, in fact eventually lost off Weymouth, through, it is believed, incorrect operation of the hangar doors.

Although floatplanes and flying boats were basically simpler than land based aircraft, largely due to the elimination of the undercarriage, their performance was usually inferior, due to the extra drag of floats or, in the case of flying boats, the hull. An increasing problem was to provide adequate clearance from the water for the propellers, which were tending to get bigger and bigger. On monoplane flying boats the clearance was obtained by making the hull deep. This provided the internal cabin space so popular on flying boats, but the penalty was high drag in flight.

An interesting attempt to overcome this problem was a Blackburn aircraft equipped with a retractable planing bottom. Blackburn originally proposed the construction of a small retractable-hull fighter, but this idea was not taken up by the Air Ministry. Blackburn then designed a bigger machine using the same principle, to meet the requirements of an official specification.

The result was the B.20, a medium-size, high-wing cantilever monoplane of all-metal construction powered by two Rolls-Royce Vulture engines each developing 1,284 kw (1,720 hp). The planing bottom, or pontoon, was divided into five water tight compartments, the centre one of which served as a fuel tank. The bottom was attached to the main hull by a system of links and when retracted fitted snugly to present a small profile of good streamline form. The main hull contained a bomb aimer's position in the bow, a large flight deck for two pilots, navigator, wireless operator and flight engineer, a galley, work room and rest cabin with a bunk. No defensive armament was fitted, but provision was made for installing powered dorsal and tail gun turrets. Mooring operations were conducted from the pontoon, which housed more equipment such as the anchor, winch, boat hook and drogue. To stabilize the aircraft with the pontoon extended, retractable floats were fitted which when retracted formed end plates to the wing.

The B.20 flew for the first time early in 1940 and during a number of subsequent flights no trouble was experienced with the retractable hull. However, the engines, selected because of their high power, were not fully developed and before high speed trials could be made the aircraft crashed due, it is believed, to engine failure. The promising idea was not developed any further.

While this development of European military seaplanes was taking place, similar activity was evident on the other side of the Atlantic. Like those of Britain, the American flying boats produced during the immediate post war period were practical rather than spectacular. Intended for coastal patrol duties, they were usually twin-engined biplanes.

Typical of these was the Boeing PB-1 (P for Patrol) built in 1925 to a Navy requirement for a flying boat capable of flying the 3,860 km (2,400 miles) from California to Hawaii non stop. Construction was primarily of metal, the top of the hull being wood and the wings being covered with fabric. The designation was changed to PB-2 when the Navy removed the tandem Packard engines and installed Pratt & Whitney Hornet air-cooled radials.

Military floatplanes included the Boeing NB-1 primary training biplane and the Boeing TB-1, produced in 1927. The TB-1 had folding wings, to assist accommodation on warships, and the float strut arrangement

Parnall Peto leaving the M2

permitted a 790 kg (1,740 lb) torpedo to be carried on an external rack under the fuselage.

In the early thirties shipborne reconnaissance aircraft included aircraft such as the Vought-Sikorsky *Kingfisher* and the Curtiss *Seagull*. A distinctive feature of these seaplanes, and also of some Japanese aircraft of the period, was the long, single, central float and small wing tip floats.

One of the most important US developments started in 1929, when the Consolidated Aircraft Corporation produced an advanced military monoplane flying boat named *Admiral*. Lack of Naval funds during this period of economic depression prevented a Naval order and so Consolidated produced a civil version, named the *Commodore,* small fleets of which were operated by the New York, Rio and Buenos Aires Line, and Pan-American Airways.

In its turn, from the *Commodore* was developed an improved military

Grumman I2F Duck, US Navy amphibian

version, designated P2Y, which went into service with the US Navy. This P2Y flying boat was the direct forerunner of one of the most famous military flying boats of all time, the PBY, or *Catalina*, which first flew in 1935. The *Catalina* had a long graceful hull, with a strut-braced parasol wing, and was powered by two 896 kw (1,200 hp) Pratt & Whitney Twin Wasp radial engines.

The feature which made the aircraft a military success was its very long range of 5,000 km (3,100 miles). This enabled the *Catalina* to go almost anywhere in the world, and proved a major advantage over the vast expanse of the Pacific Ocean during World War Two for which many hundreds were built.

The flying boat which advanced the American art of military marine craft most significantly during this inter war period however was the Martin *Mariner,* the prototype of which first flew in February 1939.

The Martin company was well suited to produce a good military aircraft, having already built many Navy patrol boats as well as some of the best passenger flying boats for Pan American. The *Catalina* had been designed around the most powerful engine available in 1935. By 1939 engines of much greater power were within sight, giving promise of a big jump in performance and armament. Accordingly, Martin chose two of the new 1,120 kw (1,500 hp) Wright Cyclones to power their new patrol bomber. To lift the engines and propellers above the bow wave and spray during rough-water operations, the company adopted a distinctive 'gull wing'. An even more distinctive feature was the unusual inward tilt up the twin fins and rudders. On the prototype the tailplane was flat, but as a result of trials it was given the same high dihedral angle as the centre section of the wing. Strangely, however, the fins were kept at right angles to the tailplane, hence their sharp inward tilt.

Planned defensive armament comprised single 0.30 in guns in the nose and tail, single 0.50 in guns aimed from transparent blisters in the side similar to those on the *Catalina*, and twin 0.50 in guns in a dorsal turret. Its range promised to be even greater than that of its rival, the *Catalina*.

The *Mariner,* together with the *Sunderland*, represented the peak development of large military patrol flying boats between the wars. Both were to be extensively used in the tragic years that lay ahead.

5 FAMOUS FLYING BOATS

Flying boats, like other kinds of aircraft, have attracted their share of machines which have been unusual, unsuccessful, very big, extremely small, or just famous.

Few have been more unusual, or less successful, than the Caproni Model 60 of 1919. During World War I, the Italian designer Gianni Caproni produced a number of large bombers and small flying boats. With the return of peace he turned his attention to the creation of a veritable leviathan of the skies — a giant flying boat intended to carry 100 passengers across the Atlantic. This may seem a modest venture in this age of jumbo jets, but at that time the idea of either a hundred-seater, or of an aeroplane capable of flying across the Atlantic stirred the imagination. To try and. produce a single craft capable of accomplishing both was almost beyond comprehension and, as it proved, certainly beyond the technological skills available at the time.

To accommodate his large number of passengers Caproni designed a huge houseboat-like hull and to lift them he used uniquely three sets of triplane wings, each supported by dozens of struts and braced by miles of wire. According to one air historian the result would *"not have looked out of place sailing up the English Channel with the Spanish Armada in 1588"*.

To power his huge aircraft, Caproni installed eight 297 kw (400 hp) American Liberty engines, four at the front pulling and four at the rear, pushing. The front two centre engines were mounted as a pair in the same nacelle and were connected to a single propeller. The nacelles for the single outer engines extended the full length of the hull, passing through the centre set of wings to join up with the nacelles of the outer engines at the rear. The

71

Caproni Ca 60

purpose of the long nacelles was two-fold; one, they were intended to brace the ungainly sets of triplane wings, and two, they provided a walk-way for mechanics to move up and down so that they could service the engines in flight.

The flying "houseboat", known as the Ca 60, was launched on Lake Maggiore in January 1921. The very first hop indicated what should have been apparent during the design stage — that the machine was extremely unstable, due to the absence of any tail surfaces.

In spite of the warning signs, ballast equal to the weight of sixty passengers was loaded into the hull and the young test pilot, Signor Semprini, was instructed to make a test flight up to a height of 18 m (60 ft). Taxi-ing out to the middle of the lake, Semprini opened up the eight engines to full throttle and, surprisingly, the ungainly machine actually left the water and made a hop flight slightly above the surface of the water. On its second flight, the huge aircraft actually climbed to about 18 m (60 ft), at which height either the machine stalled, or some of the ballast shifted, causing the nose to dip. The centre set of wings snapped and folded upward causing the aircraft to plunge back into the lake. Incredibly, test pilot Semprini survived. Equally incredibly, plans were made to rebuild the machine, but before work started the wreckage was destroyed in a mysterious fire . . .

Another flying boat which has earned itself a firm niche in aviation history is the German Dornier Do-X. Designed in 1927, this was also a big aircraft, and also intended to carry up to 100 passengers across the Atlantic.

The Do-X was the ultimate development of a long line of successful smaller Dornier *Wal* flying boats, described elsewhere in the book. Successive aircraft retained the same basic configuration, that is a boat-like fuselage, sponsons, and a slab wing on top of which the engines were mounted, the series merely growing in size. The power problem was solved by adding more engines.

When the Do-X was launched in 1929 it was a truly impressive sight. The 40 m (131 ft) long hull had the bows of a sleek cabin cruiser, and an impressive row of portholes extended almost to the stern. The wings had a span of no less than 48 m (157 ft 5 in) and empty, the huge craft weighed 27,670 kg (61,000 lb). The cockpit, or flight deck as it would be called today, was mounted on top of the hull, ahead of the wing, and accommodated a pilot and co-pilot, navigator and radio operator. Flight engineers were also carried to attend to the engines, which could be reached in flight by crawling along inside the thick wing.

The hull contained three decks, and passengers boarding the craft first passed along a corridor lined with doors that opened into little sleeping cabins. They then entered a luxurious lounge, fitted with a deep pile carpet and fine furniture, including a gramophone for the passengers to play in flight. There was also a 'recreation room', a bathroom, a smoking room, a kitchen, and a small dining room. The Do-X promised passengers travel combining the speed of an aircraft with the comfort of an ocean-going liner.

Easily the most distinctive feature of the Do-X was its powerplant — comprising no less than twelve engines mounted as six pairs on top of the massive wing. Originally, 372 kw (500 hp) Siemens Jupiter air-cooled engines were installed, but they did not provide sufficient power, and were replaced by more powerful Curtiss Conquerors. However, this change did not improve the power situation as much as had been hoped, for the aft six engines overheated, which caused a loss of power whichever type of engine was fitted.

On 12th July 1929, after some three hours of taxi-ing, all twelve throttles were opened up fully and, to many people's surprise, the huge craft took off and climbed majestically. On that exciting day, the Do-X at least proved that it could fly.

Controlling the engines presented some problems, as the throttles were operated by the flight engineer, whose station was some distance away from the pilot. In fact, between the two was the navigator's compartment and the radio room. Thus, during flight, there was considerable dashing to and fro as power setting instructions were relayed from the captain.

As a publicity stunt it was decided to conduct a weight lifting exercise, and so arrangements were made to carry 150 passengers and the crew of 10 on a sight-seeing flight round Lake Bodensee. Arranged for 31st October 1929, the huge flying boat took off without any trouble, made the flight and then landed safely — when it was discovered that in addition to the authorised 160 passengers and crew members on board, it had actually lifted up 10 stowaways as well!

Designer Dornier was obviously delighted with the aircraft, although at its gross weight of 55,790 kg (123,000 lb), its speed was only 185 km/h (100 mph) compared with the estimated 213 km/h (115 mph). To publicise his aircraft further, Dornier planned a visit to the New World. Accordingly, on 5th November 1930, the Do-X took off from the Bodensee and set course for Lisbon, its first stop. On this flight no passengers were carried; instead a good cargo of mail was on board. After Lisbon, the craft visited the Netherlands and England, where during one flight the Prince of Wales took the controls for a time.

The Do-X then set course for Portugal for the start of its South Atlantic

Dornier Do-X over Statue of Liberty

crossing. On the way thick fog was encountered and the captain demonstrated one advantage of this type of aircraft by landing in the sea and taxi-ing over 100 km (60 miles) on the surface to the haven of Bordeaux.

Misfortune then dogged the big boat. After reaching Lisbon, a fuel tank fire severely damaged one wing, which took a month to repair. Later, while attempting to take off in a choppy sea from Las Palmas, in the Canary Islands, the hull suffered damage which took three months to repair. Leaving Las Palmas, the next stop for the Do-X was the Cape Verde Islands. To prepare for the 2,590 km (1,400 miles) leg to South America, the boat was then lightened of all expendable furniture and equipment — and half the crew. Despite this, after taking off the aircraft could not gain altitude and flew most of the way as low as 6 m (20 ft) above the surface of the water, making use of the phenomenon known as 'ground effect', by which significant lift is obtained.

However, the arrival of the big aeroplane in South America could hardly fail to attract attention, and the crew were given a hero's welcome when they landed off the coast of Brazil — eight months after setting out from Germany!

The Do-X then spent some time giving pleasure flights up and down the coast of the continent, impressing all those who flew in her. The only awkward moments occurred when anybody asked questions about the big craft's performance and its fuel consumption, which was no less than 1,818 litres (400 gallons) an hour!

After flying as far south as Rio, the Do-X then turned north and followed the established Pan Am flying boat route up through the West Indies to Miami, Florida, and then on to New York harbour, which was reached on 27th August 1931. Upon its arrival here the crew were treated to one of the city's famous ticker-tape parades and a be-medalling ceremony by the Mayor. At New York the Do-X went into dry dock for an inspection, while Dornier tried hard to find a buyer for his big flying boat. There was none and so, on 19th May 1932, the Do-X took off from Manhasset Bay and, via Newfoundland and the Azores, flew home to Germany. The only incident on the return journey was that when approaching Portugal fuel ran short and so the craft touched down 10 km (6 miles) from the coast and taxied the rest of the way.

Two more Do-Xs were built, powered by Fiat engines, and sold to Italy. But, because of their very high fuel consumption, they were not profitable commercially. Thus, they were then handed over to the Italian Air Force and used for experimental purposes for a while, before being broken up.

The original Do-X was displayed in the Berlin Air Museum until it was totally destroyed during a bombing raid during World War Two.

Dornier Do-X

Providing a complete contrast with the Do-X is the single-seat Short *Cockle* of 1924. Built for Mr Lebbaeus Hordern of Sydney, this tiny aircraft was powered by two 12 kw (16 hp) Blackburn Tomtit motorcycle engines and, with a wing span of only 10.36 (34 ft) was one of the smallest and lowest powered flying boats ever built. It was also the first all-metal flying boat, being based on the pioneering all-metal stressed-skin Short *Silver Streak* of 1919. The *Cockle* was the first flying boat built by Shorts and was thus the ancestor of the many fine civil and military flying boats produced by this company.

Perhaps the most famous flying boat project to reach the prototype stage was the one conceived originally in May 1942 by Henry J. Kaiser. This American industrialist had revolutionised the ship building industry with his simple, standardised, '*Liberty Ship*' cargo-vessels.

At the time however, in the middle of World War Two, German U-boats were sinking *Liberty* ships almost as fast as they were being launched, often within sight of the American shore. To overcome this menace Kaiser suggested that a huge fleet of no less than 5,000 flying boats should be built to carry munitions to Europe.

To do the task of the ships, even this vast number of flying boats would have to have an enormous payload capacity. A transatlantic range was, of course, a basic requirement and the aircraft would also have to be able to fly safely through all types of weather. It was in impressive dream even for America where, at that time, the challenge of size seemed a catalyst for success.

Even for a man of Kaiser's vision and engineering capacity, the design of what was virtually a flying *Liberty* ship, was too difficult for him to tackle personally. So he did the next best thing. He wondered if Howard Hughes, the multi-millionaire Texan who lived for flying, would design the prototype of the huge flying boat for him, after which he would mass produce 5,000 of them.

He did not know that Hughes himself was thinking along similar lines, although at that time his experience of building even small aircraft was somewhat limited. This minor inconvenience did not stop Hughes from meeting Kaiser, who readily agreed to form a joint company to design and build the flying boat.

By October the design of the Hughes-Kaiser HK-1, as the aircraft was designated, was finalised sufficiently for a weight breakdown and performance summary to be submitted to the U.S. War Production Board. Less than a month later a contract was signed for the manufacture of three HK-1s, one of which would be used for static testing.

The general appearance of the HK-1 was deceptively simple. Of

Short Cockle

conventional, single-hull, high-wing layout, the only immediate indication of its size was the row of eight Pratt & Whitney Wasp Major engines mounted neatly along the leading edge of the massive 97.53 m (320 ft) span wing. Looking somewhat like thimbles from a distance, the engines were in fact 28-cylinder radials, with four banks of staggered cylinders and developing something over 2,232 kw (3,000 hp). The huge hull, over 61 m (200 ft) long, could carry a 60-ton heavy tank or any other vehicle in the U.S. Army inventory. Alternatively, it could be fitted with seats and equipment for no less than 700 infantrymen.

In order that the huge flying boat would not divert men and scarce materials from the war effort, the government stipulated that the project must not syphon off any trained engineers from war plants and that it should use Duromold and other non-critical materials as much as possible. Duromold was a patented method of building double-curvature structures by moulding resin-impregnated plywood in a powerful, hot press. The snag was that the technique had only been tried out on small samples.

Fortunately, apart from certain areas of the skin, much of the structure did not have double curvature so that there was no need to employ the Duromold process everywhere. Most of the structure was of laminated birch, because the flying boat was basically a wooden aeroplane. Because of this the aircraft earned the nickname the *'Spruce Goose'*.

Building even quite small aeroplanes in wood presents many problems that do not arise if metal is used; the building of the biggest aeroplane in the world in this material was a painstaking and difficult engineering task. It was also a lengthy one, compounded by the eccentricities of Hughes which, even at this early stage of his life, were adversely affecting his management capabilities. Kaiser left after a particularly thunderous row, and when in 1944 it was discovered that manufacture had barely started, the Army Air Force and Navy also withdrew their support for the project. Hughes continued work on the giant flying boat alone.

It was not until October 1947, long after the war which it was supposed to help win had ended, that the *Hercules*, as the flying boat was now named, was ready. In view of the long delays in completing the aircraft, many people did not believe that it would even fly or, if it did succeed somehow in taking off, that it would crash immediately. However, when the *Hercules* was towed from the large dry dock in which it had been built, some of the criticism was stilled, first because of its majestic size and secondly because of the smooth manner in which it rode the choppy sea.

Hughes made two fast taxi-ing runs to get the feel of the flying controls and the sit of the aircraft on the step as it all but flew. On the second run, the left wing float dug deeply into the water causing some of the watchers to think that Hughes had lost control. What he was doing in fact, was deliberately letting the float trail in the water, and act as a brake, to help him turn sharply and miss a boat which had steered across his path.

Returning to the starting point, Hughes opened up the eight engines again, this time to full power. The huge craft accelerated slowly, but was soon up on the step and moments later was clear of the water. Flying at a height of about 9 m (30 ft), Hughes travelled approximately two kilometres (1 mile) before closing the throttles and gently alighting amid a cloud of spray and to the thunderous cheers of the crowd on the shore.

Rather sadly, but perhaps fortunately in view of the doubts about the airworthiness of the craft, this short flight was the only one ever made by the *Hercules*, even though it was later fitted with more powerful engines. But, even if it had flown again and fulfilled all its performance expectations, it would not have been followed by thousands of sister flying boats because, with the ending of the war, the need for them had long since gone.

The *Hercules* is, however, undoubtedly one of the most fantastic flying boats ever built. In the story of aviation generally, it remains today one of the happier tributes to Howard Hughes, without whose drive, enthusiasm and money, it would never have been built. In the story of flying boats it nearly realised the dream of those early visionaries who envisaged a future when the skies would be filled with fleets of giant flying ships.

6 THE GOLDEN AGE OF FLYING BOATS

By 1930, pioneer flyers had laid the foundations for a series of air routes, from North America to South America and across the Pacific, and from Britain to Africa and the Far East. Pioneer designers had, meanwhile, laid the foundation for a new generation of flying boats and seaplanes.

In the United States, the ten-seat Sikorsky S-38 was followed by the forty-seat S-40. Introduced in November 1931, this had a longer range than any other aircraft then in operation, and was the first of a long line of 'clipper' airliners to serve with Pan American.

To Sikorsky, the big S-40 with its wing span of 34.74 m (114 feet) was a *'thing of joy and beauty'*, but to Charles Lindbergh, then technical adviser to Pan American, it was, because of its incredible array of struts and bracing wires supporting the wings and engines, more like a *'flying forest'*.

Only three S-40s were built, but these made more than one thousand flights in a little over two years, achieving an on-time arrival record of a remarkable 99 per cent, a figure few airlines achieve today despite the technical advances that have been made since then in both aircraft design and navigational aids.

These three rather obsolescent flying boats were followed by the more important, longer range and much more beautiful, S-42. On this aircraft the four neatly cowled Pratt & Whitney Hornet engines were installed directly into the leading edge of the wing, this feature alone drastically reducing the number of struts and bracing wires, while the wing itself was attached to the hull by a slender streamlined pylon. The wing, of more advanced aerodynamic planform, embodied flaps to provide additional lift at take off and to assist braking when landing. But the innovation which contributed

Sikorsky S-42

decisively to the performance of the S-42 was the installation of variable
pitch propellers, so that maximum efficiency could be obtained during both
take-off and cruise conditions. The beautifully sleek hull could
accommodate up to 32 passengers in great comfort. Its fine looks, however,
were more accident than a primary requirement of design, as the Pan
American order of priorities was: passenger safety, followed by efficiency
and trouble-free operation, payload and performance were the first
considerations. The lack of looks as a formal requirement, however, did not
prevent many people considering the S-42 to be the most beautiful aircraft
of its time.

   With a range of 3,860 km (2,400 miles), a top speed of 300 km/h (188
mph) and useful passenger carrying capacity, the S-42 is often regarded as
the first true flying boat airliner produced in the United States. In April
1934, the new aircraft demonstrated its potential by setting no less than ten
world records for payload, altitude and speed.

   With the S-42, Pan American began to initiate services across the Atlantic
and Pacific Oceans, and the intensity of airline rivalry during this period,
particularly between Pan American and Britain's Imperial Airways, is

Martin M-130 Clipper

typified by the hard hitting negotiations involved. The range of the S-42, although good, was not great enough for a direct U.S.-Europe transatlantic service. The key to this important route was the landing rights acquired by Pan American in Newfoundland, then a separate British Dominion and not part of Canada. In 1933 Newfoundland suffered a severe economic crisis and its Dominion status was cancelled, the state becoming a Crown Colony, under the direct rule of the London government. With this change in status, Imperial Airways lost no time in persuading the British government to cancel the landing rights granted to Pan American, thus effectively blocking the plans of the U.S. airline for a transatlantic service.

In planning his trans Pacific services, Juan Trippe found the British

Martin M-156 *Soviet Clipper*

equally obstructive. The keys to these long distance routes were bases on islands such as Midway, Wake, Guam, Pago-Pago, and Kingman Reef. For the Honolulu — Auckland, New Zealand, route, the tiny speck of mountain top known as Canton Island was an obvious choice. This was evident to Britain, whose Royal Navy had been reconnoitring such islands under the guise of 'fishing expeditions'.

In 1939 the U.S. erected a tiny lighthouse on this uninhabited island in an attempt to indicate ownership. Simultaneously, Britain established a solitary postal official in a wooden hut on the beach on the opposite side of the little island to demonstrate *her* sovereignty. The airline rivalry got so

Dornier Do-Wal on *Westfalen* catapult

serious that to back her claim the U.S. despatched a Navy submarine
chaser, while a cruiser from the Royal Australian Navy was sent to protect
Britain's postman. Fortunately, common sense prevailed before shots were
fired, and agreement was reached that the island would be occupied jointly
by the two countries.

Flying alongside the Sikorsky S-42s on the Pan American routes were the
equally impressive Model 130 Ocean Transport flying boats made by the
Glenn L. Martin Company. Like the S-42, the Martin aircraft evolved from
an earlier series of smaller aircraft and was one of the classic aircraft of that
time. Produced to meet a Pan American specification, the M-130 was
powered by four 670 kw (900 hp) Pratt & Whitney Wasp engines and had a
wing span of 43.3 m (142 ft). It could carry 41 passengers at 255 km/h (140
mph) and had a normal range of 5,150 km (3,200 miles), or 6,437 km (4,000
miles) if only carrying mail. Three of these beautiful aircraft, known as the

China Clipper, Phillipine Clipper and the *Hawaii Clipper,* captured the imagination of both young and old. A year after entering service the three clippers had flown 4,395,620 km (2,731,312 miles), carried 1,986 passengers and over 226,800 kg (500,000 lb) of cargo.

In 1942, the *Phillipine Clipper* and *China Clipper* were drafted into military service by the U.S. Navy, and both were used to operate a shuttle service between San Francisco and Pearl Harbour. The *China Clipper* made eighty-eight round trips in one year.

Martin built a single example of an even bigger flying boat, the M-156. It was sold to Russia and is thus known as the *Soviet Clipper. Aeroflot* expertise in keeping records is evidently not so great as the Soviet airline's undoubted skill in operating air services, as all enquiries regarding the use and ultimate fate of this particular aircraft have not been answered.

*   *   *

While the Pacific was being criss-crossed by Sikorsky and Martin flying boats, other marine aircraft were overcoming the vastness of the Atlantic Ocean. One ingenious method developed in 1933 by *Lufthansa,* the German national airline, was to catapult seaplanes from mother ships which had carried them part of the way across the ocean. Initially, the mother ship *Westfalen* was used to carry Dornier *Wal* (Whale) flying boats, which, loaded with mail, were launched as soon as the ship had taken them within range of the South American continent. Using this technique, regular air mail services were inaugurated in 1934. Later a Blohm and Voss Ha-139 four-engined float plane, launched from the mother ship *Schwabenland*, operated across both the North and South Atlantic.

Another ingenious solution to the problem of range was developed in Britain in 1937 and involved the use of a modified Short *Empire* flying boat to lift a smaller aircraft. The idea was originated by Major R.H. Mayo, who calculated that it would be possible to mount a small aircraft on top of a bigger one, and to use the power and lift of both to take off and fly towards a distant destination. The upper aircraft would be heavily laden with fuel and payload, and when on the way, would be released in flight, carrying a load that it could not have taken off with on its own. The mother aircraft would then return to base.

Known as the Short-Mayo *Composite*, the mother ship was a modified Empire flying boat, the *Maia,* fitted with a wing of increased area and the structure to support the upper aircraft. The engines were also moved outward from the centre line to ensure adequate clearance between the propeller and the floats of the upper aircraft. Named *Mercury,* this was a

86

Blohm and Voss Ha 139 on *Schwabenland* catapult

specially-designed, high-winged, four engined monoplane. Of interest is the fact that the engines of the upper aircraft were started from inside the flying boat, using compressed air. Indicator lights inside *Maia* told the pilot if *Mercury* was mounted safely on its support cradle.

Each aircraft was first test flown individually by Lankester Parker and found to have good handling characteristics and performance. These individual flight trials were followed by the first 'paired' take-off on 4th January 1938. The first in flight separation was made on 6th February, the *Maia* flying boat diving gently, and the *Mercury* climbing to ensure adequate clearance between the two aircraft. The test flight was a complete success.

The first transatlantic crossing was made on 21st July. The Composite took off from Foynes in Ireland, with *Mercury* carrying an enormous load of mail, newspapers and fuel. Flying well out to sea, the two aircraft separated cleanly. *Maia* returned to Foynes, and *Mercury* flew safely to Montreal covering the 4,715 km (2,930 miles) in a flight of 20 hours 20 minutes.

Blohm and Voss Ha 139

Short Mayo Composite aircraft taking off

This was the first non-stop aeroplane flight between Britain and the Canadian capital. The flight also broke the record for the East-West Atlantic crossing and also gained the distinction of being the first *commercial* crossing by virtue of the 453 kg (1,000 lb) payload carried by *Mercury* on the occasion.

In October of the same year *Mercury* flew non-stop from Dundee to the Alexander Bay, South Africa, a distance of 9,652 km (5,998 miles), setting a seaplane distance record that was not beaten for many years. On 29th November 1938 the *Composite* inaugurated a non-stop mail service between Southampton and Alexandria, Egypt. With a flight time of only nine hours, the service continued regularly until the outbreak of World War Two.

Although the Short-Mayo *Composite* was one answer to the problem of achieving long range with a heavy payload, it was only suitable for the carriage of freight and mail. It was not suitable for scheduled passenger services. Nor was the in-flight refuelling technique, developed by Alan Cobham's *Flight Refuelling Ltd*. Using Handley Page Harrow tankers, this technique was used to enable two Empire flying boats, *Cabot* and *Caribou*,

Short Mayo Composite aircraft about to separate

to operate a mail service between Southampton and New York. This was the first time the scheme had been attempted as a commercial proposition and it proved highly successful, but was not practical for passenger services.

* * *

Deserving a mention in this account of the golden age of flying boats are two crossings of this great ocean accomplished by massed formations of flying boats.

The first such crossing was made by fourteen Italian Savoia-Marchetti SM 55 flying boats. Led by the Italian Air Minister Marshal Italo Balbo, these set out from Rome on 17th December 1930 to cross the South Atlantic and ten eventually arrived at Rio de Janeiro on 6th January 1931. Originally designed as a torpedo bomber, the SM 55 was of a most unusual twin-hulled

Short Calcutta at Westminster, London (1928)

Short Empire flying boat *Canopus*

configuration, with an open cockpit and very thick wings. It was powered by two engines mounted back to back above the wing and canted upward at a striking angle. A formation of no less than 24 SM 55s set out from Rome on 1st July 1933 to cross the North Atlantic on the occasion of the World's Fair being held that year. The huge armada, divided into eight flights of three aircraft, was again commanded by Balbo.

Journeying via Amsterdam, Londonderry, Reykjavik, Cartwright, New Brunswick, Montreal, the destination Chicago, the host city for the Fair, was reached on 15th July 1933. Apart from a mishap to one aircraft, which was replaced at Amsterdam, all twenty-four aircraft arrived safely. After visits to Washington and New York, the return flight, also in formation, was made via the Azores. In spite of strong headwinds and overheating engines, the aerial fleet, escorted by fifty seaplanes of the *Regia Aeronautica,* arrived home in perfect formation to be greeted by the Italian dictator Mussolini in person and the cheers of thousands of proud Italian people.

The Short *Singapore* flying boat used by Sir Alan Cobham for his African survey flight was a military aircraft, and its service exploits are therefore described in the next chapter. From it, however, was developed first the superb three-engined fifteen passenger *Calcutta* and then the bigger

Short Empire beaching operation

four-engined Short *Kent*. The *Kent* could carry 16 passengers, 362 kg (800 lb) of baggage and no less than 1,360 kg (3,000 lb) of mail, and three of them operated the Mediterranean section of the Imperial Airways' London-to-India service.

Although not so fast as comparable landplanes, the spacious flying boats were very popular with passengers, and in 1935 Imperial Airways took the unusual step of ordering a complete fleet of no less than twenty-eight new Short flying boats, to be used exclusively on all their Empire air routes.

The order was a big gamble, as the new aircraft were to be the first four-engined, all-metal monoplane flying boats ever built. The new aircraft, known as the *Empire* flying boats, were powered by four 677kw (910 hp)

Short Empire promenade

Short G-Class *Golden Hind*

Bristol Pegasus engines, and could carry seventeen passengers with their luggage, and two tons of freight. While cruising at 264 km/h (164 mph) they had a range of 1,300 km (810 miles). Their top speed, 322 km/h (200 mph), was as high as that of many fighters of the day.

The prototype *Canopus* first flew on 4th July 1936 and went into service on the Imperial Airways trans-Mediterranean service on 30th October 1936 — less than four months after its first take-off.

The rest of the fleet was launched at the rate of about two a month, and by 1937 the fleet was flying over 182,171 km (113,196 miles) on the airline routes yearly.

The rivalry between Pan American and Imperial Airways to be the first airline to operate regular passenger services across the Atlantic was intense. The likely traffic between New York and the capital cities of Europe was immense and the potential reward, in both prestige and revenue, enormous. In 1937, however, the two great airlines came to an agreement for a joint transatlantic service. The 'small print' of the agreement stipulated that no American airline could start such a service unless Imperial Airways could offer a similar service.

Pan American, with its S-42, had an aircraft which could just fly from the

Boeing 314 Clipper

Boeing 314 Clipper base

North American continent to Britain, providing the wind was helpful. To match this two Empire class flying boats, *Caledonia* and *Cambria*, had their fuel capacity increased to give them a range of up to 6,080 km (3,780 miles).

Both airlines then had suitable aircraft of a kind and on 5th July *Caledonia* set out from Foynes, Ireland, and covered the 3,110 km (1,933 miles) to Botwood, Newfoundland, in 15 hours 8 minutes, while the Pan American Airways flying boat, *Clipper III* made a simultaneous crossing in the opposite direction in 12 hours 34 minutes. These were the first airline flights across the North Atlantic in history, but they were somewhat of a freak. The range of the S-42 was not sufficient for it to cross the ocean regularly in all weathers, while although the modified Empire flying boats had the range, they could not carry any payload!

What was needed was a flying boat with the range of *Caledonia* and the payload of the S-42. To meet this challenge Short produced three 'G'-class flying boats, designed specifically for the Atlantic service.

Each of these three 33-ton aircraft, *Golden Hind, Golden Fleece* and *Golden Horn,* were powered by four 1,027 kw (1,380 hp) Bristol Hercules engines and combined a cruising range of 5,150 km (3,200 miles) with unprecedented standards of comfort and luxury.

On the other side of the Atlantic, Boeing produced the Model 314 *'Clippers'*. These magnificent aircraft, designed to meet a specification issued by Pan American early in 1936 for a long-range four-engined flying boat, represented a peak in pre-war airliner development. Powered by four 1,116 kw (1,500 hp) Wright Twin Cyclone engines, the sleek but spacious hull could accommodate no less than 74 passengers in great comfort, at a speed of 296 km/h (184 mph) over ranges up to 8,367 km (5,200 miles). They went into service across the Atlantic in June 1939 and soon set new standards of travel on this most difficult air route.

In addition to their service on the North Atlantic, these magnificent flying boats added new laurels to their reputation for dependability on the transPacific, to San Francisco to Hong Kong route.

The Short G-class aircraft and the Boeing 314 Clippers represented the end of two decades of hard airline route pioneering and of flying boat development. Both aircraft had the range, payload and reliability to be commercially viable, and the comfort and speed to attract passengers. With regular services across the North Atlantic being operated by Boeing Clippers, the last great air route had been conquered. But before the G-class had even entered service, and only a few months after Pan American's Boeings went into service across the Atlantic, Britain was at war with Germany.

When the war ended five long and bloody years later, fundamental changes in aviation development made it impossible for this graceful form of air transport to flourish.

7 FLYING BOATS AT WAR — WORLD WAR II

The pioneering bravery of pilots together with the pioneering skill of manufacturers in the twenties laid the foundations for the golden age of flying boats in the thirties.

This era of graceful, reliable and safe air travel was, with the inauguration of scheduled passenger services across the North Atlantic by Pan American, reaching a new peak of effectivity, when war once again broke out in Europe.

Surprisingly, the transition from peace to war had, at first, little effect on civil flying boat operations. In Britain, the main Imperial Airways base at Southampton was moved to Poole, but the airline's flying boat services continued much as before — twice weekly to South Africa and Karachi, once to Kisumu in Kenya and three times a week to Singapore. It even managed to start some new ones, to New Zealand, in April 1940, and later to Canada, so that all the British Dominions were then linked to the Mother Country.

The route to Canada, operated by the Empire flying boats *Clare* and *Clyde,* was in fact a leg of the first British passenger air service across the North Atlantic to New York. The account of how *Clare* arrived in New York on her fourth trip, while the Battle of Britain was at its height, complete with newspapers telling of the Royal Air Force's important victories, is one of the great stories of the war.

The civil operations continued even when, in June 1940, Italy's entry into the war effectively closed the Mediterranean to British ships and aircraft. Contingency plans were put into operation by British Overseas Airways (formed when Imperial Airways combined with British Airways) to keep

B.O.A.C. Boeing 314 being serviced

open the vital Empire routes. Durban, in South Africa, replaced beleaguered Britain as the Western terminal of the flying boat route to India and Australia. The contingency plan joined together at Cairo the two Empire routes from Britain to South Africa and Australia, to form a single great horseshoe-shaped route linking Durban with Sydney, via East and Central Africa, Khartoum, Cairo, Palestine, Iraq, the Persian Gulf, India, Burma, Siam and Singapore. Britain itself was connected to the new route by a landplane service through France, French North Africa, across the Sahara Desert and on to Khartoum. Sixteen Empire flying boats were east or south of Alexandria in early June 1940, and these were diverted to South Africa for operation on the new route. Within only nine days the 'Horseshoe' service was being run once weekly in each direction, and after

101

Dornier Do 24

six weeks the frequency was doubled. The operation was a great credit to the management skill and dedication of the B.O.A.C. staff — and to the reliability of the flying boats involved. It continued until February 1942 when the fall of Singapore to Japanese forces broke the 'Horseshoe' and severed Australia's air link with Britain.

*   *   *

During this period other civil flying boats which performed well included the Boeing 314s. These beautiful aircraft had only just entered service when the war forced route changes, disrupted schedules and caused many of them to be 'called up' for military service.

Like their military counterparts, civil flying boats in the Pacific were caught unawares when Japan attacked Pearl Harbour in December 1941. The *Pacific Clipper,* on the San Francisco to Aukland run, had just landed at the New Zealand terminal when the Japanese assault started. To avoid the risk of flying home over potential enemy waters, the flying boat was instructed to return to the United States the long way — via Australia, India, Arabia, central Africa, South America and then to New York, a distance of no less than 55,520 km (34,500 miles).

Another 314 made an even longer flight. It was planned that the 314 *Anzac Clipper* should pick up President Roosevelt at Casablanca to fly him, Prime Minister Churchill and Premier Stalin to Australia for a conference with the Chinese leader Chiang Kai-shek. The meeting was cancelled at the last minute because it was believed that Japanese intelligence had got to know of the rendezvous, but the Captain of the *Clipper* continued with the original flight plan, taking instead a General and his staff to Australia. By the time the *Clipper* had returned to New York it had flown round the world and covered 59,108 km (36,728 miles). It was the first flying boat intended for commercial use to accomplish this.

Without doubt the most distinguished pilot to fly a Boeing Clipper did so in 1942, when BOAC's *Berwick* flew Winston Churchill from a meeting with Roosevelt from Norfolk, Virginia to Bermuda. Later Churchill wrote *"I took the controls for a bit to feel this ponderous machine of thirty tons or more in the air. I got more and more attached to the flying boat."*.

Churchill should have completed his journey to Britain aboard the ship *Duke of York* but, learning that the 314 had sufficient range, decided to fly home in the *Berwick*. During the long night flight the flying boat strayed off course. Some time after Lands End should have been in sight but wasn't, the pilot, Captain Kelley-Rogers, decided to turn north sharply. It was fortunate that he did so, because another six minutes of flying on the original course would have taken the flying boat and its cargo of V.I.P.s right over Brest — then a major base for German U-boats and surrounded by anti-aircraft guns.

Even then the 314 was not clear of trouble. Coming in from the South, the flying boat was picked up by a radar station in Kent and logged as an "Unidentified Aircraft". Half-a-dozen Hurricanes from Fighter Command were scrambled to shoot it down. Fortunately they failed to locate it and the flying boat landed safely with its precious cargo at Plymouth.

*   *   *

With three-quarters of the world covered by water and with Britain dependent upon sea routes for her survival, it was obvious that flying boats

Dornier Do 26

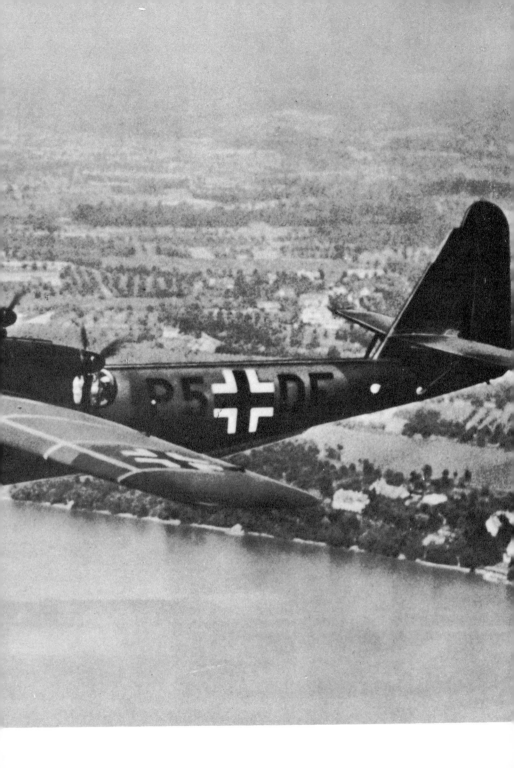

Blohm and Voss Bv 138

would be heavily involved in military operations, and this proved to be the case.

In Europe, although most of the combatants had flying boats in military service, only Britain employed them in a decisive fashion.

France had the biggest complement of flying boats when the war started, but most of these were either obsolescent or obsolete, and had little military impact upon the events leading up to that country's fall.

Germany, with little interest in extensive overwater operations, nevertheless had the Dornier DO-18, DO-24 and DO-26, and the Blohm and Voss Bv138, the latter designed specifically for long-range reconnaissance. Do-26s were used as transports during the Norwegian campaign, although they were easy victims for fighters. The Bv 138 was also used as troop transports during this campaign.

During the war, Blohm and Voss produced two new flying boats, the Bv

Blohm and Voss Bv 222

222 and the Bv 238. Appearing in 1940, the Bv 222, was designed initially for use over the Atlantic by *Lufthansa*. Powered by six engines, it would have carried 24 passengers in airline service. During the war it was used for reconnaissance and as a transport ferrying supplies to Rommel in North Africa, in which role it could carry 90 soldiers. The even bigger Bv 238, an ambitious multi-role aircraft with a wing span of nearly 61m (200 ft), appeared in 1944. It was destroyed by Allied fighters while engaged on its development trials.

Russia, like Germany, had little interest in marine operations. However, it is estimated that as many as 1,500 of the single-engined Beriev MBR-2 short range reconnaissance aircraft were produced. The MBR-2 was followed by the bigger, improved, MDR long-range flying boat for operations over the Baltic, Black Sea and the Pacific.

At the outbreak of war Britain had exactly one hundred military flying boats in service at home and overseas, but only 41 were modern monoplanes, 39 of these being *Sunderlands* and two *Lerwicks*.

The remainder were biplanes in various stages of obsolescence, including twenty-eight *Londons,* seventeen *Singapores* and fourteen *Stranraers*. These biplanes were retired fairly quickly.

In the Atlantic theatre the U-boat threat was such that the main task of flying boats, and indeed of all Coastal Command aircraft, was the suppression of submarines attacking the convoy routes.

U-boats, which had nearly given Germany victory in the Great War by sinking some 5,000 ships totalling eleven million tons, came nearer to gaining victory over Britain than is generally known in the Second World War also. In the Great War Britain avoided defeat at the eleventh hour by introducing, in May 1917, the convoying of her merchant shipping, after which only about 250 ships were sunk out of some 84,000 sailings.

In 1940, in spite of this experience, Britain underestimated the threat posed by the U-boats, partly because she assumed only a small German fleet and partly because the development of *Asdic,* for detecting a submerged submarine, led her to believe that U-boats would be far more vulnerable than they had been previously.

Not only did both assumption and belief prove to be wrong, but Britain was even more dependent on sea commerce than she had been in 1914. Britain's population had increased by nearly four million between wars, and

Blohm and Voss Bv 222 over unfamiliar environment

Blohm and Voss Bv 238

her survival depended upon her ability to import about half her food
requirements, eight million tons of timber for use in her coal mines and
twelve million tons of oil. The latter need had increased ten-fold between
the wars, while Britain's tanker fleet had fallen from one half to one quarter
of the world's total.

*   *   *

However, in one respect Britain did learn from the experience gained during
the early war, and the convoy system was put into operation at once. As the
convoys approached Britain, the U-boats' main killing ground in the early
months of the war, they were met first by *Sunderlands* patrolling up to 580
km (360 miles) from their bases in Wales, Devon, Cornwall and the
Shetlands. The *Sunderland* patrols, along with those of other aircraft of
Coastal Command, pushed the U-boats away from the shores of Britain. As
the U-boats were forced further and further out into the Atlantic, so the
flying boats followed them, operating from new bases in Iceland and West
Africa.

    Coastal Command's flying boat squadrons were well suited to such work,
as a *Sunderland* could patrol for up to 16 hours and a *Catalina* for up to 27.

Short Sunderland nicknamed flying 'porcupine'

However, the all-time record for a single operational sortie must surely go to Air Commodore 'Kelly' Barnes and his *Sunderland* crew who, it is recorded, once stayed out for seven days! This apparently impossible patrol was achieved as follows. Having patrolled for a time, without sighting anything hostile, the captain put the flying boat down in mid ocean in the hope that a U-boat might come within range. After a while, the crew resumed their patrol, then alighted again and so on, until after seven days of such activity it was considered time to return to base. It is unfortunate that this initiative was not rewarded by an attack on a U-boat.

Many military flying boats of this period were poorly armed and easy prey to enemy fighter action. Not so the *Sunderland*. This aircraft was heavily armed, with power operated gun turrets at the bows and stern, and so many beam guns that the *Luftwaffe* nicknamed it the flying "porcupine". The flying boat had only one major vulnerable spot, its underside, and pilots often prevented attack from this quarter by flying very low down over the water.

In addition to its primary bombing-reconnaissance role, *Sunderlands*, as indeed did all flying boats, often carried out rescue missions to ships in distress or airmen who had come down in the sea. *Sunderlands* also engaged in mine laying operations in ports along the European coast used by the Germans.

Sunderland operations were handicapped in the early stages of the war by the inadequacy of their depth charges and by the lack of detection aids. The only way to detect a submarine during this period was by eyes alone. This was difficult under operational conditions and impossible at night or in bad weather. Long patrols were also very fatiguing; during one mission the Captain reported, solemnly, that he had just seen a man riding a bicycle on the surface of the sea.

When, by luck, a U-boat was spotted, they were surprisingly difficult to destroy. The standard British 113 kg (250 lb) anti-submarine depth bomb was such a poor weapon that even a direct hit did not guarantee the destruction of a U-boat. Matters were made worse by the fact that the bombs were set to explode at 22 fathoms, at which depth they were unlikely to hit anything and certainly did little harm to a U-boat on or near the surface.

However, the value of the *Sunderland*, and other anti-submarine aircraft, as an anti-U-boat weapon cannot be indicated by the number of German craft sunk, but rather by the number of Allied merchant vessels it helped to keep afloat. The saving (or sinking from Germany's viewpoint) of even one ship was the equal of winning a significant ground battle in terms of the equipment involved, as indicated by the following figures. A typical cargo for an average 6,000 ton merchant ship was 21 tanks, four six-inch howitzers, 44 small field guns, 12 armoured cars, 25 Bren carriers, 2,600 tons of ammunition, 300 rifles, 200 tons of tank spares and 1,000 tons of miscellaneous stores.

The development of improved depth charges and that of radar equipment that could detect a surfaced U-boat first at 8 km (5 miles) and then 32 km (20 miles) drastically reduced the number of U-boats on station near Britain, forcing them ever further out into the Atlantic. The U-boats then engaged the convoys in the area, out of range of shore-based aircraft. This unpatrolled area, known as the 'Atlantic Gap' was not covered until the delivery of the U.S. Liberator towards the end of 1941.

The main U-boat killing ground, however, was not the mid-Atlantic, but the Bay of Biscay. British Operational Research had determined that it was

Consolidated PBY Catalina

much easier to detect the German craft in this transit area, than in the open Atlantic. Accordingly a determined offensive operation in this area was intiated in 1943, and between May and August 28 U-boats were sunk and another 22 damaged.

In May, the attacks in the Bay of Biscay and others elsewhere, sank no less than 41 U-boats, over a quarter of Germany's operational strength. For each U-boat lost during this month the Germans sank only 4,500 tons of Allied shipping; one year earlier the ratio had been 60,000 tons for each U-boat lost. Such losses were intolerable and the Germans withdrew most of their U-boats from the Atlantic.

The Battle of the Atlantic had been won although many more ships were to be sunk and many more men lost, before the war ended. When it did end, over 14 million tons of British and Allied shipping lay at the bottom of the sea, together with the remains of 1,069 U-boats, including 284 scuttled by

Catalina taking off with RATO rockets

the Germans. Coastal Command aircraft accounted for more than two-thirds of all the U-boats sunk. Between 1939 and 1945 flying boats had evolved from a harassment force into the most effective anti-submarine weapon of the war.

*　　*　　*

As the *Sunderland* was the backbone of Britain's military flying boats, so was the Consolidated PBY *Catalina* the backbone of the U.S. Navy's. Compared with the *Sunderland,* the *Catalina* was very poorly armed, with

113

Martin Mariner

only two hand-operated machine-guns in large perspex observation blisters, one each side of the hull aft of the main cabin. It was also very slow, having a top speed of only 209 km/h (130 mph), and very uncomfortable. However, its very long range, 5,000 km (3,100 miles) made it a valuable weapon indeed for operations over the vast expanses of the Pacific Ocean.

Catalinas actually went into action before the Japanese attack on Pearl Harbour. One hour before this attack started a *Catalina* on patrol assisted in sinking a Japanese submarine behaving suspiciously in the waters near Pearl Harbour. At the time the pilot of the *Catalina*, Ensign William P. Tanner, feared he had sunk one of his own craft, as he landed at his base at Kaneohe, about 32 km (20 miles) east of Pearl Harbour. The main *Catalina* base was on Ford Island, and all doubts about the identity of the submarine vanished when, just before 8.00 a.m. the Japanese attacked the *Catalina* bases with dive bombers. Of the thirty-six aircraft at Kaneohe, all were destroyed or damaged except three that were airborne on patrol.

For many months the best that the *Catalinas* could do was to provide as much warning as possible of further Japanese advances. This advance reconnaissance sometimes paid big dividends, as it did when Ensign Jewell Reid, at the controls of a *Catlina*, gave the first news of elements of the Japanese fleet on the way to attack Midway. The advance warning alerted all American forces for the ensuing battle which, when it was over, had ended all hopes of Japan's conquest of the Pacific.

Although slow and poorly armed, the *Catalina* was a very reliable and rugged aircraft, and nowhere were these two characteristics more essential than in the Aleutians. This string of islands stretching down from Alaska, was invaded by Japan as a diversion for their major attack on Midway. The areas around the islands were usually foggy, gusty and always freezing and the nearby mountains covered with mist. The cold was such that the engines often had to be heated before they could be started, and a ditching in the sea meant death from exposure unless rescue came very quickly. One of the perils of the region were *williwaws,* the name given to a local wind which could, suddenly, reach a velocity capable of overturning aircraft.

The second most widely used U.S. flying boat was the Martin *Mariner.* Like most aircraft of its kind its initial promising performance, particularly its range, had been progressively reduced by the installation of more and more equipment, but the installation of 1,562 kw (2,100 hp) Double Wasp engines increased its speed to 346 km/h (215 mph) and enabled its full load of 3,630 kg (8,000 lb) to be carried for more than 4,345 km (2,700 miles). This was despite the fact that the normal defensive armament now consisted of no less than eight 0.50 in guns in three turrets and two waist hatches.

Nearly 1,400 *Mariners* were built and they were engaged in many acts of

Martin Mars, heavy weight transport

skill and bravery. The former included the rescue in 1942 of nine survivors from the torpedoed British tanker *Arcadio*. This rescue was accomplished despite the presence of U-boats and 3 m (12 ft) waves. The following year another *Mariner* rescued all 48 survivors from the stricken *Cape San Juan*. The flying boat, in fact, with its ability to alight on the sea, was a unique weapon in that it was said to have saved during the war the lives of as many servicemen as it caused casualties to its enemies.

It was in the Atlantic that the *Mariner* most heavily engaged its main adversary — the German U-boat. Several *Mariners* engaged U-boats while they were surfaced. These were not the one-sided battles that might be assumed, as many U-boats were armed with eight 20 mm cannon for defensive purposes, and a skilfull crew could have these manned within ten seconds of the conning tower breaking the surface.

The *Mariner* was not the first or only flying boat to alight on dry land — as one did on the bed of Willcox Dry Lake. It must have been the first one, however, which after such a landing, was inspected, found to be airworthy — and promptly flown out again.

Boeing Sea Ranger, military flying boat swan song

Another 'first' achieved by the *Mariner*, and another indication of its ruggedness, is that it was the first flying boat to be fitted with RATO (rocket assistance take-off). For this, four rocket units were attached in pairs beneath the wings, angled to help push the aircraft up as well as along.

The Japanese, being an island race, also used flying boats, although the bulk of their aircraft development had been concentrated on fighters. At the time of Pearl Harbour, the Japanese Navy had only one long range flying boat in service, the Kawanishi Type 97, code named *Mavis* by the U.S. Like most Japanese aircraft of the period, it lacked protective armour for its crew, defensive guns, and its fuel tanks were not self-sealing. It was thus extremely vulnerable to fighter fire, to the extent that it was withdrawn from daylight operations in the middle of the war.

The *Mavis* was superseded by the much improved Kawanishi Type 2, code named *Emily*. With a wing span of about 38 m (125 ft) it was the biggest flying boat produced by Japan and with a top speed of nearly 483 km/h (300 mph) was the fastest flying boat of the war. It had an impressive maximum range of 6,438 km (4,000 miles). It was defended by no less than five 20 mm cannon and four 7.7 mm machine-guns, and was fitted with self-sealing fuel tanks. All round, it was one of the finest military flying boats of the war.

However, it was no match for the U.S. fighters such as the Republic *Thunderbolt* and North American *Mustang* which began to appear in the Pacific towards the end of the war, and of the 167 *Emilys* built, all were destroyed except one. This sole survivor was sent back to the U.S. for a study of its hydrodynamic and flying characteristics.

But, as the golden age of civil flying boats came to an end with the beginning of the war, so the golden age of military flying boats closed with the end of the war.

With the proliferation of airfields throughout the world, the need for aircraft capable of operating from water bases diminished. The writing on the military flying boat wall began, perhaps, with the launching of the Boeing XPBB-1 *Sea Ranger* in the middle of 1942. This was an advanced, twin-engined, ultra-long-range flying boat and, with a wing span of 42 m (139 ft), was the biggest of its type in the world. It was armed with eight machine-guns, could carry up to 10 tons of bombs, depending on the range, and, so it is claimed, could remain on patrol for up to 72 hours. To build this wonder plane, Boeing erected a special plant at Renton. But, in the event, only one *Sea Ranger* was built. The huge Renton plant was used instead to build the *B-29 Superfortress* landplane bomber. The *Sea Ranger* was the first of many flying boats to fall to a superior landplane, for land-based military aircraft were faster, could lift heavier loads and carry them further, and were more cost effective in the pursuit of war.

8 AGE OF DREAMS

In spite of the remarkable record of flying boats before and during the last war, the advance of landplane technology together with the changed climates of economics and politics brought about by prolonged world war, was inexorably ensuring their decline and eventual extinction. In the military field, the cancellation in the middle of the war of the advanced Boeing *Sea Ranger* long-range flying boat in favour of the even more advanced B-29 *Superfortress* was an indication of things to come.

Another indication was given by the special committee, set up in the middle of the war by Britain under the chairmanship of Lord Brabazon, to determine what type of aircraft were likely to be needed by British operators when peace returned. When the Committee published its conclusions these detailed no less than seven types of airliner and freight aircraft — but not one of them was a flying boat!

Lord Brabazon explained the reason for this omission several years later in a personal letter to the author;

"At the time we could find no operators who would express themselves in favour of flying boats, just as nobody would favour liquid-cooled engines. This being so we were unable to put it down as an agreed recommendation. I need hardly say that our own views were different, but we were asked to do a particular job and it would have been outside our terms of reference to make a recommendation which had not been required by the users."

Thus, despite the preference of many people who travelled by air, and that of many of its own members, the Brabazon Report virtually sealed the fate of British civil flying boats.

* * *

B.O.A.C. Hythe class Sunderland conversion

The cancellation of the Boeing *Sea Ranger* and the Brabazon Report does not mean that no new military flying boats were developed or that civil flying boats were not used after the war, or indeed, are not still being used today.

While British Overseas Airways ordered new fleets of American four-engined landplanes, such as the Lockheed *Constellation* and Douglas DC-4, for use on the prestigious North Atlantic route, the airline continued to use flying boats on its Empire routes with their well-established chains of marine bases. In fact, during the months immediately after the war, flying boats were even used on the North Atlantic route, until the landplanes were ready. This service was operated by the Corporation's three famous Boeing 314s, the *Berwick, Bristol* and *Bangor,* which had survived the war and were still going strong. By the summer of 1945 these aircraft were operating this demanding service at the extraordinary rate of 3,467 flying hours a year. This number of flying hours means that they were airborne for nearly ten

121

Sandringham, in Funchal harbour, Madeira

hours every day. The turn round time at Poole, after their flight from Baltimore, was just two hours. Such an annual utilisation and turn round time would be creditable today — in 1945 they were testimony to the reliability of the flying boats and the dedication and skill of those who flew and maintained them.

For the Empire routes BOAC used a fleet of twenty-one Sunderlands converted into 22-seat airliners, known as the *'Hythe'* class. These proved to be among the most comfortable air transports in operation at the time. Other boats used by BOAC in the post war period included the *Sandringham,* a civil development of the *Sunderland,* and the *Solent.*

Seating up to 45 passengers, the *Sandringhams* were used to supplement *'Hythes'* on services to Singapore, Japan and Johannesburg. *Sandringhams* were also used by the Argentine Dodero Company, and Norwegian Airlines DNL. The Norwegian company introduced their fleet of three on the *'Route of the Midnight Sun',* from Stavanger, Bergen, and Oslo to Trondheim, and then to Bodo, Harstad and Tromso, well inside the Arctic circle. This route was considered by many seasoned travellers as the most beautiful air route

122

in the world, combining breath-taking views of the terrain, sun and sky. At the time the *Sandringham* was the biggest airliner used on any domestic air route in Europe.

The *Solent,* the last of the large commercial flying boats, was a long-range civil derivature of the *Seaford* which, in turn, had evolved from the *Sunderland.* Powered by four 1,257 kw or 1,503 kw (1,690 hp or 2,020 hp) Bristol Hercules engines, the *Solent,* could carry up to 42 passengers, and had a maximum range of 4,830 km (3,000 miles). It was luxuriously appointed and included a library and cocktail bar on the upper deck, and a ladies powder room!

The *Solent* was used by BOAC on routes to Johannesburg, the Far East and Australia. When the flying boat was replaced by landplanes on these routes, Tasman Empire Airways used them on the busy 2,090 km (1,300 miles) Auckland to Sydney route linking New Zealand with Australia. In time too, however, this route was operated by the more efficient landplanes. All British commercial flying boat operations ceased in 1958. As far as British Airways was concerned, the age of the flying boat had ended.

* * *

On the other side of the Atlantic, Pan American also phased out flying boat operations, not without sadness among the crews who flew them and the ground crews who serviced them. The necessities and advances of the long war meant that aircraft, market competition and techniques had taken or were to take on a new face. The exciting age of route pioneering was largely over, but new challenges lay ahead.

During the war the backbone of the airline's Latin American services was the fleet 21-seat Douglas DC-3, well known as the Dakota. However, seven S-43 amphibians served on services to the Brazilian interior, and a lone, ageing Junkers W34 single-engined seaplane remained in use for services along the Magdalena river. At least one of Pan American's S-42s was stripped of 1,140 kg (2,500 lb) of passenger fittings, to begin an all-cargo service in 1941 initially on the Miami Canal Zone route, and by 1943 into South America as far as Brazil. The flying boat had a cargo capacity of some 3,630 kg (8,000 lb) and used for Pan American's first regular, scheduled all cargo operations outside Alaska.

At the end of the war Pan American, like BOAC and other intercontinental airlines, found itself able to make use of a ready-made, world-wide system of land airports, most of them featuring prepared runways and fully equipped to handle the first post war generation of four-engined landplanes. Unlike BOAC, however, the U.S. airline did not have

Short Solent, Tower Bridge, London

Princess 100-seat flying boat

to wait long for the delivery of converted long-range military transports, or newly-built airliners of the same models.

No time was lost in phasing out the remaining flying boats, which had become expensive to operate and were beginning to show their age. Apart from the existence of landplane facilities, further flying boat development was out of the question for airline purposes, on account of the high operating costs of these aerodynamically inefficient aircraft, their unsuitability for certain winter operations through surface icing, and their inability to serve most inland towns and cities.

Pending the delivery of the new landplane aircraft, the Pan American transatlantic services, were maintained through most of 1945 by the Boeing 314 *Clippers*. As the airline's new Douglas DC-4s were delivered, so were the flying boats phased out of service. The last to fly on the Atlantic routes settled down onto the water to end the service on 6th January 1946, followed shortly afterwards by those on other routes. There was no further use for this one-time fine aircraft. Most of them, including the bulk of the

B-314s and the four remaining S-42s, suffered the ignomity of ending their days in the breaker's yard. In January 1946 the Dinner Key flying boat base was closed.

*　　*　　*

Over the Pacific, operations between San Francisco and Honolulu had been resumed on 16 November 1945, using B-314 Clippers. The final Pan American B-314, last of the magnificent old flying boats, was retired from the Hawaii service on 8th April 1946, its place being taken by the new Lockheed 049 *Constellation*, which cut the flying time on the San Francisco to Honolulu route from 17½ hours to 9¾ hours.

Thus ended the era of operations on which Pan American was founded, perhaps not a highly efficient one commercially, but one accomplishing great achievements and providing safe, comfortable and reliable service.

Although the operation of flying boats after the war has been on a diminutive scale compared with that of landplanes, this does not mean that manufacturers did not have ideas for new marine craft that made this period more an Age of Dreams than an age of actual aircraft.

One such dream, conceived during the war, was the project by Howard Hughes and Henry Kaiser for a "flying *Liberty* ship". In Britain, in spite of the Brabazon Report and the preference of operators for landplanes, another dream was the Saunders-Roe SR-45 project of 1945. This 100-seat, six-engined, 3,220 km (2,000 miles) range airliner was impressive by many standards. The wing span was 67 m (220 ft), the hull 44.5 m (146 ft) long with a beam of 4.88 m (16 ft). The depth of the two-deck hull was 7.3 m (24 ft) and was of characteristic double-bubble cross-section to facilitate hull pressurisation.

An innovation was a patented automatic docking system. Once down on the water all the pilot had to do was to taxi between two marker buoys, when a mooring cable was automatically engaged and the aircraft winched into its berth. Powered flying controls promised to make the massive aircraft easy to fly and the cabin pressurisation would further enhance the traditional luxury of flying boats. The giant flying boat was to be powered by six 3,735 kw (5,000 hp) turboprop engines.

Project SR-45, named the *Princess*, promised to combine Britain's demonstrated skill in the difficult art of building large flying boats with her pioneering lead in the new turbine powerplant field. Unfortunately, this was not to be. A major problem was that there were no engines available that were suitable to take the place of the "paper ones" drawn so neatly in the nacelles protruding from the wing leading edge.

127

Duchess jet flying boat project

By 1948, however, a solution seemed to be at hand — the 2,615 kw (3,500 hp) Bristol Proteus being developed for the Brabazon 2 landplane airliner. It was proposed to use ten of these engines, in four coupled pairs with two single engines in the outer positions. The total of 26,150 kw (35,000 hp) was all the power, and more, that the designers required.

Initially, it was hoped that the *Princess* would fly in 1949, but this date slipped first to 1950, then to 1951. It was not until August, 1952, that the great boat finally made its majestic first flight. At this time, however, a major snag was that the Proteus engines, instead of developing the hoped for 2,615 kw (3,500 hp), were giving only 1,870 kw (2,500 hp). Thus, instead of providing an extra 3,735 kw (5,000 hp) total, they were delivering 3,735 kw (5,000 hp) less. Plans to fit *Orion*, and later *Tyne,* engines also failed to materialise.

Even sadder, was the fact that, due to government mismanagement, there was no keen prospective operator waiting to operate the flying boat. B.O.A.C. were lukewarm, to say the least. At one time the Royal Air Force was said to be interested. The best bet of all was an offer in 1953 from British Aviation Services, who had taken over Aquila Airways operating the only flying-boat service from Britain at the time, from Southampton to Madeira, to buy the three *Princesses* built for £1 million each. This offer was not accepted. Had it been, there is little doubt that the Princess would have been popular with passengers and more than likely profitable for Aquila Airways. Unfortunately, this was not to be. It seemed as if the British Government, although not able to use the aircraft itself, was determined not to let anyone else try in case they succeeded.

Another dream which never materialised was that of the *Duchess*. Also conceived by Saunders Roe, the *Duchess* was a projected 925 km/h (500 mph) 74-seat flying boat, powered by six de Havilland *Ghost* pure jet engines installed deep inside gracefully swept wings. Incorporating the most advanced aerodynamic and hydrodynamic features, the *Duchess* held promise of doing for British marine craft what the *Comet* was doing at the time for land-based airliners. Tasman Empire Airways expressed sincere interest in the *Duchess* for use on its route linking New Zealand and Australia. Unfortunately, the keen interest of one operator was not sufficient to launch the project, and another dream died.

An even greater dream, for the far future, was a Saunders-Roe 'feasibility study', prepared in the early fifties, for a really big flying boat, intended to carry 300 passengers and 40 tons of freight across the Atlantic. This 500-ton marine giant had a triple-bubble hull and was shown powered by eight 9,335 kw (12,500 hp) engines driving contra-rotating propellers, four mounted on the leading edge and four aft of the 97 m (318 ft) span wing.

129

Short Sealand amphibian

Of course, it was never intended that this particular flying boat should be built. It was merely an ambitious feasibility study to determine if such a large marine aircraft would be practicable. The study showed that it was, at a time when a 500-ton landplane would have been quite unthinkable. Twenty years passed before the Jumbo Jet landplane became a reality.

Not all British plans for flying boats remained dreams. One project that actually matured into a flyable aircraft was the Short *Sealand* of 1946.

The uses to which this little boat was put, typify the value of an aircraft that needs no prepared landing ground. Apart from its basic use for normal passenger-carrying on feeder services, the aircraft was used for air survey work, air/sea rescue and ambulance duties, forest and anti-fire patrol, ice patrol, and whaling work. Not all the inhabitants of the Earth live as close to cities or means of transport as do the great majority of the readers of this book. During the immediate post-war years the inhabitants of many of the outlying or inaccessible parts of the world found it increasingly difficult to keep pace with the general speeding-up of communications between the

130

Hythe class flying boat and the *Queen Mary* liner. Both were made obsolete by land planes

better developed regions. The *Sealand* helped them to 'keep up with the Jones' in places as far apart as Borneo, Yugoslavia and Norway. However, useful as the little *Sealand* was, it played an insignificant part in the general development of civil aviation during this period.

As in the case of military flying boats, civil landplanes were more efficient than their water-borne counterparts. Technically, the weight and problems of designing and housing an undercarriage were less than those involved in developing an aerodynamically efficient hull as speeds increased. The advent of pressurised cabins also posed greater problems on flying boats.

But, even if efficient turbo-jet, swept-wing flying boats could be built, their operation for the mass carriage of millions of passengers would obviously pose problems for which there is no real answer.

131

One only has to watch the scenes on the apron of a busy international airport such as Charles de Gaulle, Heathrow or New York, to realise that flying boats could never be operated in the numbers and frequency of landplanes. The problem of surface freezing in winter is also one for which no practical solution has been offered.

It would also be apparent that the large numbers of servicing vehicles needed to ensure the rapid turn round of a large airliner, could not readily be replaced by waterborne counterparts.

In the same way that the exciting age of steam locomotives has gone on the railways, it must be accepted that the graceful age of large passenger-carrying flying boats has also gone.

9 POST WAR MILITARY DEVELOPMENTS

When Japan surrendered in 1945, military aircraft development did not end with quite the abruptness that it did so after the signing of the Armistice in 1918. This was due partly to governmental plans for a more orderly transition to peace, and partly to the fact that, although a great war against evil had just ended, the world was not necessarily a peaceful or safer one. The Russian blockade of Berlin in 1948 demonstrated this sad fact and was the harbinger of events to come. Thus, in spite of the increasing comparable superiority of landbased aircraft, funds continued to be allocated to the continued development of marine aircraft, in Britain and the U.S.A., and to a lesser degree, Russia.

During the war the development of and the potential uses of the jet engine, were not unnoticed either by the designers of flying boats or by their service users. The war in the Pacific had demonstrated the need for air superiority during the vital landing periods as Allied troops laboriously retook the islands in that ocean overwhelmed by the Japanese during their campaigns of 1942. The need for a fighter was apparent and the idea was conceived for one which could be deployed when no airfield was available.

Thus in 1944 Britain issued a specification for a single-seat, twin-jet fighter flying boat for use in such areas. Of interest is that four years previously the Japanese Navy had issued a specification for a single-seat fighter seaplane to cover the early phases of amphibious landings and for the defence of small islands where hard runways were impractical! The result of this specification was a float-plane development of the exceptional 'Zero' fighter, the appearance of which was one of the more unpleasant shocks given to the Allies during the initial stages of the war in the Pacific.

133

Saunders-Roe SR/A1, world's first fighter flying boat

In the British specification the application of the jet engine to a marine aircraft held promise of eliminating some of the inherent features of seaplanes which placed them at a disadvantage when compared with high performance landbased aircraft. These were, principally, the high thrust line required by propellers, the poor aerodynamic shape for high speeds of a hull which had adequate water performance, and the relatively high structure weight of a hull compared with a landbased fuselage.

When conceived, the revolutionary British aircraft was specifically intended for the Pacific war, but in the event the war did not develop as anticipated and consequently the construction programme of the SR/A1, the designation of the aircraft, was slowed down. The new fighter was designed around two Metropolitan-Vickers Beryl turbojets. These engines, the first British axial-flow engines, developed up to 1,746 kg (3,850 lb) thrust, and were small in diameter compared with the centrifugal type favoured by other aircraft manufacturers at that time. Two, therefore, could be installed side-by-side without making the beam of the hull unduly great. The intake was provided with an extendable lip which was intended to overcome water ingestion troubles, although this in fact was not needed. The engine exhausts exited at the trailing edge of the wing root and were splayed out 5 degrees each side of the centre line.

Because of the leisurely pace of the development programme, it was not until June 1947 that the SR/A1 flew, when its graceful hull of faired Vee-form was displayed to advantage for the first time. With a top speed of over 800 km/h (500 mph), its peformance approached — but did not quite equal — contemporary landbased fighters such as the *Meteor* and *Vampire*. This was amply proved during the 1948 Farnborough Show when the Saunders Roe test pilot, Geoffrey Tyson, gave a superb display of aerobatics including some really spectacular low inverted flying that no-one who saw it is ever likely to forget.

The aircraft was armed with four 20 mm cannon mounted in the top of the hull ahead of the pilot, to eliminate any harmonisation difficulties. In addition, either two 450 kg (1,000 lb) bombs or eight rockets could be carried.

Only three SR/A1s were built. One was lost when the pilot, practising for a local air display in bad weather, crashed into the sea. A second was lost when it struck a half-submerged baulk of timber just after touching down. The loss of the two aircraft, plus the fact that exports were unlikely, brought the SR/A1 programme to an end.

Tests were resumed with the third aircraft for a short period in November 1950, when the Korean War had indicated the usefulness of a fast, heavily-armed flying boat operating in support of naval and ground forces. This aircraft is now preserved in a museum.

The SR/A1 represented a valiant attempt to harness jet propulsion to a marine aircraft. Although the aircraft performed well in isolation, it was still outclassed by contemporary landplane jet fighters and it was by no means a practical weapon system. The twin problems of refuelling and re-arming quickly under operational conditions were never tackled satisfactorily.

Another determined effort to close the superiority gap between landplanes and water-borne aircraft was made by Convair in the United States. This effort culminated in the *Sea Dart*, a delta-winged, hydro-ski fighter even more revolutionary than the SR/A1. It was the ski which singles the American project out for sheer technological innovation. In an attempt to produce a competitive aircraft, the Convair designers decided that it was not just a matter of reducing the frontal area of the hull; any increase in aerodynamic drag due to waterborne requirements had to be eliminated completely. The floats or hulls of previous sea-borne fighters were to be replaced by skis.

135

Convair Sea Dart ski fighter

Basically, the conception was simple because in principle the skis worked exactly like those people put on their feet for fun. However, in practice getting the skis to work satisfactorily on aircraft proved difficult. Among several aircraft used for full-scale flight trials was a Grumman *Goose* which, in the late 1940s, flew with a variety of ski configurations with encouraging, but what proved to be misleading, results.

When the *Sea Dart* was finally completed in December 1952, its appearance revolutionised all previous concepts of naval aircraft. It had a normal fuselage, an amazingly thin 60-degree delta wing, with a similar shape for the tall single fin and rudder. Indicative of the high speeds hoped for was the Vee-shaped windscreen. There was no conventional flat panel, but two acutely sloping side windows which formed a sharp vee in front for minimum supersonic drag. Power was provided by two Westinghouse turbojet engines mounted side-by-side above the wing, with the inlets just aft of the leading edge. When at rest water lapped over the tips of the wing, making it seem as if the aircraft was in the process of sinking! Two skis were

136

Martin Marlin, served in Korea

embodied, and these extended and retracted on shock absorbing struts rather like a conventional retractable undercarriage.

A protracted series of taxi-ing trials was necessary before the Sea Dart made its first flight in April 1952. In the air the *Sea Dart* was quite impressive, but the engines were a continual source of trouble and the twin-ski arrangement proved unsatisfactory. However, the overall concept was sufficiently promising for the U.S. Navy to place an initial order for 12 production fighters in August 1952. These were to have a single central ski, because flight trials with such an arrangement had proved more successful on the second prototype, which was modified to this configuration. In August 1954 the YF2Y-1 became the first seaplane to exceed the speed of sound, which it achieved in a shallow dive. However, disaster struck three months later when the aircraft burst into flames and disintegrated when making a high-speed run during a public display. The accident caused the Navy first to postpone its evaluation and then to cancel the entire programme in 1956. Thus ended, perhaps for ever, the quest for a seaplane fighter with landplane performance.

Developments of less innovative military flying boats were more successful. A new concept of hull design in the United States by the Martin Company was embodied in their P5M *Marlin* in 1948. This had a slender hull, the reduction in frontal area giving the twin-engined aircraft a performance comparable to its land-based contemporaries. The basic advantage, of being able to operate from unprepared sites was not, of course, impaired. In those days, at the height of the 'Cold War', this was considered important in the event of a communist attack on the Allies world-wide network of land bases.

Although, perhaps fortunately, the *Marlin* was never subjected to the supreme test of a world-wide conflict, the flying boat took part in the Korean War. The flying boat also saw service in Vietnam, where its duties included patrolling the thousand-mile South Vietnamese coastline in an attempt to identify and harass the supply of war material to the Viet Cong. The *Marlin* had a range of over 3,200 km (2,000 miles) and could cover a great deal of water during a single patrol. Its independence of prepared bases was well demonstrated for, with the support of a single seaplane tender and several small boats, many *Marlins* were water-based away from their home station for as long as two months at a time.

Of slightly earlier vintage was Britain's *Shetland*, the first prototype of which flew in December 1944 and the second in September 1947. Work on this aircraft was actually initiated in 1940 to meet a specification calling for a four-engined, long-range reconnaissance flying boat capable of carrying a 1,800 kg (4,000 lb) bomb load and heavy defensive armament. At the time the *Shetland*, with a wing span of 45.72 m (150 ft), was the biggest British flying boat ever built. By the time the aircraft flew, however, many changes had taken place in operational requirements and the aircraft was not fitted with military equipment. In addition, the performance of the machine left much to be desired, particularly regarding control characteristics. Trials were halted by the loss of the first prototype by fire at its moorings in January 1946. The second aircraft was completed as a civil transport, with accommodation for forty passengers, but this was eventually broken up without seeing either military or civil service.

More promising was the Short *Seaford*, a development of the famous *Sunderland* and, indeed, initially known as the *Sunderland Mk IV*. The flying boat embodied many innovations, the chief of which was the installation of four 1,344 kw (1,800 hp) Bristol Hercules engines, making it superior to its wartime predecessor in all respects. It had a cruising speed of 333 km/h (207 mph) and a maximum endurance of 15 hours. Thirty *Seafords* were ordered, but the number was subsequently reduced to six with the ending of the war in the Pacific. These served for a short period with No 201 Squadron, R.A.F., but were afterwards converted for civil use and renamed *Solent*.

More successful was Convair's new concept for big flying boats, the XP5Y-1. Designed for Navy patrol duties, this slender craft was powered by

Convair Tradewind

four Allison turboprop engines driving six-bladed propellers. The prototype flew early in 1950 and subsequent trials revealed more-than-expected 'bugs', particularly in connection with the engines. The aircraft suffered an accident in 1953 and was destroyed.

The project was re-evaluated by the Navy and developed into a transport with the new designation R3Y. Given the beautiful name *Tradewind*, eleven of these impressive aircraft were built and used by the Navy on runs such as that between Almeda and Pearl Harbour. This version could carry 80 passengers in rearward facing seats, up to 24 tons of cargo or an assault company of Marines more than 3,200 km (2,000 miles) without refuelling.

A special cargo version, designated R3Y-2 and sometimes known as the *'Flying LST'* embodied an upward opening nose to facilitate the loading and unloading of troops and equipment. Although the *Tradewind* was used for a variety of tasks, including an aerial tanker for air-to-air refuelling, and proved the practicability of high-speed flying boat transports, production did

Convair Tradewind unloading a howitzer

not extend beyond the original order as no further funds were allocated to the type.

To carry the development to its logical conclusion and utilise turbojet power, Convair proposed a jet-propelled flying boat successor to the Navy, but the contract was awarded to their traditional rival, Martin. Building upon their success with the *Marlin,* Martin produced what is undoubtedly the most sophisticated flying boat ever constructed. If there ever was a seaplane destined to take marine aviation into the future this, the P6M *Sea Master,* was surely the one to do so.

To the slender hull concept developed for the *Marlin,* Martin married a sharply swept wing, similar to those being installed on advanced landplanes of the period. Power was provided by four Allison turbojets, mounted in pairs on top of the wing, to keep the intakes clear of spray when alighting and taking off. The wings, spanning 30.50 m (100 ft) had anhedral and this, combined with the sweepback, brought the wings almost down to water level, enabling the stabilising floats to be mounted on the tips.

The long slender hull contained a bow radome, a pressurised crew compartment, a large central weapons bay and various rear compartments. The bombs and mines were mounted on a rotary bomb door, of the type developed by Martin first for the XB-51 bomber and then for the B-57 development of Britain's *Canberra.* The single door was a bomb rack and door combined. It was pivoted on the centreline at the front and rear, and driven by a rapid actuator which could rotate it upside down in a second. When inverted the bombs or mines attached to its inner face could be released. On the door could be mounted up to 13,600 kg (30,000 lb) of stores, which could include a large reconnaissance camera pod. The huge door was made watertight by inflatable rubber tubes.

The *Sea Master* made its first flight in July 1955 during which all went well. Flight trials continued during the summer, when speeds in excess of 966 km/h (600 mph) were claimed. Progress was encouraging when, during a flight on 7th December, the one thing the flying control designer feared most happened. The actuator controlling the trimmer on the variable incidence tailplane 'ranaway', that is, it drove the surface to the limit of its travel. The huge aircraft, travelling at high speed, pitched down sharply. The engines tore away from the wings, which, under the high airloads, bent down and actually touched beneath the hull, before the aircraft broke up, killing the crew of three.

Trials continued with the second prototype, but during special vibration checks, this too went out of control and executed a tight loop before breaking up. On this occasion, happily, the crew managed to escape from the stricken aircraft.

142

Martin Sea Master

A major redesign programme followed this mishap, during which the wing was given dihedral in place of the former anhedral. Other changes included the installation of more powerful engines, the jet pipes of which toed out sharply. Most important, a new, all-transistorised auto-pilot and flight control system was installed.

This major effort is more readily understandable if one recalls the contemporary political situation prevailing in the U.S. At that time the Navy had dreams of creating a strategic Seaplane Striking Force (SSF), to help rival the global influence of the U.S. Air Force Strategic Air Command. This concept was described by the then Assistant Secretary of the Navy for Air, in the following terms:

"Also promising, I think, is the long-range attack seaplane. This has an additional advantage which the carrier force lacks — they can be widely dispersed overseas in many small, relatively inexpensive, units, in areas

143

Beriev M-12 Seagull taxies past a Beriev M-10, surviving only as a monument

where maintenance of other forces would be too costly. Two or three seaplane squadrons in an area thousands of miles from American soil could maintain a threat to an entire flank and require a diversion of enemy defenses from other fronts, without exposing vulnerable fixed bases to an enemy's counter attack. Failure to exploit this advantage would leave an enemy able to concentrate his forces in areas closest to the targets he seeks in the United States. With perhaps half a dozen seaplanes, a single tender, and a pair of tanker submarines, we could provide an integrated force that an enemy could not ignore."

To create the SSF, the Navy had ordered an initial fleet of 24 *Sea Masters,* but through the delay caused by the redesign work and the accompanying steep rise in costs, six aircraft were cancelled. The first production aircraft flew in February 1959, and the Navy boasted how well their new aircraft could mine the Black Sea, and claimed it was "a major new anti-submarine warfare system ... able to go after enemy submarines in their home ports." However, by this time the force of 18 aircraft had been reduced to eight, which were planned to operate as a single squadron from a new 'seadrome'. In the event, even these eight aircraft proved too expensive and only three production *Sea Masters* were built.

The demise of the *Sea Master* ended not only America's development of the large military flying boats but that of the West generally. Although Britain had plans for an ambitious four-jet, swept-wing naval patrol flying boat, this never progressed beyond the project stage. The only other large jet flying boats were those which matured in the Soviet Union.

These were developed by the Beriev Bureau, which has been working on seaplanes since the late 1920s. The Bureau's first jet flying boat was the twin-engined Be-8, but it seems unlikely that this entered production. A much more advanced swept-wing twin-jet flying boat was seen for the first time in the 1961 Soviet Aviation Day Flypast, and went into service with the Soviet Naval Force in which it had the official designation M-10.

Four M-10s took part during the 1961 Flypast. The aircraft had a single-step hull, somewhat similar to that on the Martin *Marlin,* but with an even higher length-to-beam ratio. Other features of interest were an observation station in the bows, a fighter-type canopy over the flight deck, a defensive position in the tail, with radar-directed twin 23 mm guns, and a large spray-fence on each side of the nose to keep water out of the intakes, located somewhat surprisingly under the shoulder-mounted 'gull' wings. Marked anhedral on the outer sections of the sharply swept-back wings permitted the non-retractable stabilising floats to be mounted on the wing tips, as on the *Sea Master*. In 1961 an M-10 set up no less than eleven international records. Two of these, for height 14,962 m (49,088 ft) and speed in a straight line 912 km/h (566.69 mph) had not been bettered by early 1980.

However, like the *Sea Master*, the type is no longer in service. Also like the *Sea Master*, although it took seaplane technology to a new high plateau, it was still not sufficient to carry seaplanes into the seventies.

The Saunders Roe SR/A1, the Martin *Sea Master* and the Beriev M-10 represented peaks in the development of seaplane fighter, bomber and patrol aircraft respectively. They were the last in long lines of development of a class of warplane, the days of which seem to have gone forever. There is no significant place for them in a world dominated by missiles and nuclear weapons.

10 FLYING BOATS TODAY — AND TOMORROW?

Sad for many people who have experienced the tranquillity of travel in this class of aircraft, is the fact that today only three 'large' flying boats of any note are in service in the world. A much larger number of smaller float planes are used for pleasure and business, particularly in Canada where economic conditions and the presence of thousands of small lakes combine to make them a viable proposition. The number of float planes, however, is only an insignificant fraction of their land-based counterparts.

The three large flying boats in service are the Beriev M-12, of the Soviet Naval Air Force, the Shin Meiwa PS-1 of the Japanese Maritime Self-Defence Force, and the Canadair CL-214. Of interest, if not of significance, is the fact that all three of these 'survivors' are amphibians, that is, they can alight on both land and water.

The Beriev M-12 is a twin-turboprop medium-range maritime reconnaissance amphibian, the existence of which was first disclosed to the West during the 1961 Aviation Day flypast at Tushino Airport, Moscow. Thus, the design is at least twenty years old.

Powered by two 2,987 kw (4,000 shp) Ivchenko engines, the M-12 has a wing span of 29.70 m (97ft 6 in), a maximum range of 4,000 km (2,485 miles) and a cruising speed of 320 km/h (200 mph). The single-step hull has a high length-to-beam ratio and embodies a glazed observation and navigation station in the nose, and a long magnetic anomaly detector (MAD) 'sting' extends from the tail.

The wing is sharply cranked and high-set, with the engines mounted on top of the 'apexes', to provide the maximum propeller clearance. The cowlings of the engines open downwards in two halves, so that they can be

Beriev M-12 Seagull amphibian

used as servicing platforms, an engineering feature used on many flying boats from very early days.

Right from the beginning, the M-12 began to establish records. First it gained six height records, since when it has gained, and in many cases subsequently bettered, a total of 21 records. The M-12 also held, early in 1979, all 15 records for turboprop flying boats.

When three M-12s took part in the 1967 air display at Domodedovo, the commentator said that the unit to which they belonged was *"one of those serving where the country's military air force began"*, implying that the aircraft were then in operational service. Since then, M-12s have been observed in regular service at Soviet Northern and Black Sea Fleet air bases and were reported to have been operational for a period from bases in Egypt. About one hundred of the type are believed to have been built, but it is not known whether it is still in production, although this is considered unlikely. So is a replacement aircraft. Flying boats have never figured prominently in Russian aviation and the M-12 could well be the last of a short-lived breed.

The Japanese Shin Meiwa PS-1 is a four-turboprop STOL anti-

147

Shin Meiwa US-1 Search and Rescue amphibian

submarine flying boat from which an air-sea rescue variant, the US-1, has been developed. It is the most advanced flying boat in the world today.

It was in 1966, after seven years of design projects, that the company was awarded a contract to develop a new anti-submarine flying boat for the Japanese Maritime Self Defence Force (JMSDF). Two prototypes were built, the first of which made its maiden flight on 5th October 1967. Following· development trials, during which take-offs and landings were made successfully in seas with wave heights of up to 4 m (13 ft) and 25-knot winds, fifteen production aircraft were ordered. Designated PS-1, these are now in service with the 31st Air Group of the JMSDF, most of them with No 51 Squadron at Iwakuni. A further five PS-1 have been ordered.

Apart from its sleek boat-like fuselage, the PS-1 is of very conventional configuration. A surprising feature is the marked lack of wing dihedral angle, in marked contrast to the gull-wing of Russia's M-12. Sophisticated high-lift devices contribute significantly to the aircraft's STOL capability. These include leading-edge slats on the wings outboard of the engines, and large outer and inner blown trailing-edge flaps. The flaps are continuous behind the engines, so that the slipstream is deflected when they are extended. Together, these lift devices are claimed to provide nearly three times the lift of a conventional wing, giving the PS-1 a stalling speed of only 75 km/h (46 mph).

148

Canadair CL 215 utility amphibian

A novel feature is the leading-edge slats fitted to the tailplane, and both the elevators and the rudder are 'blown', like the wing flaps, to provide effective control and stability at very low speeds.

In spite of the high length-to-beam ratio of the hull, this has the ample accommodation capacity typical of flying boats. The flight deck, a feature of which is the wide-visibility bulged side windows, accommodates two pilots and a flight engineer. Aft of this on the upper deck is a tactical compartment, housing two sonar operators, a navigator, MAD operator, radar operator, radio operator and a tactical operator. Aft of the tactical compartment is a weapons compartment which houses passive long-range accoustic search equipment with 20 sonobuoys and their launchers, active accoustic echo ranging with 12 explosive charges, four 150 kg (330 lb) anti-submarine bombs, and smoke bombs. External armament includes two under-wing pods each containing two homing torpedoes and a launcher beneath each wingtip for three air-to-surface rockets.

The US-1 Search and Rescue version has accommodation for a crew of nine and up to twenty seated survivors or twelve stretchers. A sliding rescue door is fitted in the port side of the fuselage, aft of the wing. The Transport version can carry up to 69 passengers in four-abreast seating with a central aisle. The rear portion of the cabin is convertible to a cargo compartment.

In order to enhance the potential uses of the flying boat, Shin Meiwa, in co-operation with the JMSDF and the National Fire Agency, have completed a design study of a water bomber conversion of the aircraft and the PS-1 first prototype has been converted into a water bombing testbed. Trials, using tanks of 8.1 tons water load, indicated that the aircraft could deliver up to 185 tonnes (182.1 tons) of water, picked up 70 km (43 miles) from base to a site 10 km (6 miles) away, in under 4 hours. The proposed production version, with tanks of 14 tons capacity, could deliver 315 tonnes (310 tons) to a site the same distance from its base before needing to refuel.

This potential use as a water bomber, highlights a unique advantage of flying boats for this kind of operation — the ability to take on a large load

CL 215 water bombs a fire

of water quickly and to deliver this rapidly to a fire. No other type of aircraft can match the flying boat in this respect.

It is thus of interest that the last of the three flying boats under review, the Canadair CL-215, was specifically designed for fighting forest fires. It is something of a surprise that a 'mundane' matter such as forest fire fighting could even justify the attention of any aircraft, let alone one designed especially for the task. In Canada, however, forests are one of that country's great natural resources, the value of which in recent years has increased almost as dramatically as oil.

Forest fires, however, not only destroy vast areas of valuable timber. In the South of France and in Spain, as in many other parts of the world, beautiful forests are a major source of pleasure for millions of tourists, who in turn bring prosperity to the regions. A fire can be an economic disaster. Fires also upset nature's delicate balance for years and can also pose serious threats to property and human lives.

It was this combination of the affect of fires that prompted Canadair to produce the CL-215. This is a twin-engined amphibious flying boat, with a high wing, the water load being carried in two 2,673 litre (588 gal) tanks in the main hull compartment. This may not sound very much, but relatively small amounts of water are required to quench a fire if loads can be delivered at an early stage in key areas in rapid succession. That is just what the CL-215 does. On a number of occasions single CL-215s have made over 100 drops, totalling 545,520 litres (120,000 gal) in one day. Water is taken aboard, while the aircraft taxis at high speed, by two probes which extend below the surface, a full load being scooped up in 12 seconds. Fighting one fire, one aircraft made 31 drops in an hour, emphasizing the importance of scoop pick-up while taxi-ing. To drop the water load two large doors are provided in the hull bottom, which discharge the entire load in less than a second.

In Canada the Province of Quebec operates a fleet of fifteen CL-215s and they have been responsible for saving millions of dollars of timber. In France the *Securité Civile* has operated a fleet of CL-215s since 1969, and the flying boat is claimed to have reversed the trend in which that country was losing more timber annually than it was able to grow. The French aircraft have also been used to fight fires in Corsica, Germany and Italy. Other countries using CL-215s include Greece, Spain and Thailand.

Although intended primarily for fire fighting, the CL-215 is adaptable to a wide variety of other duties. A utility version can carry up to 19 passengers. In the Search and Rescue configuration, the flying boat has a navigator's station, a flight engineer's station, two observers stations and provision for either four seats or three stretchers.

De Havilland Twin Otter float plane

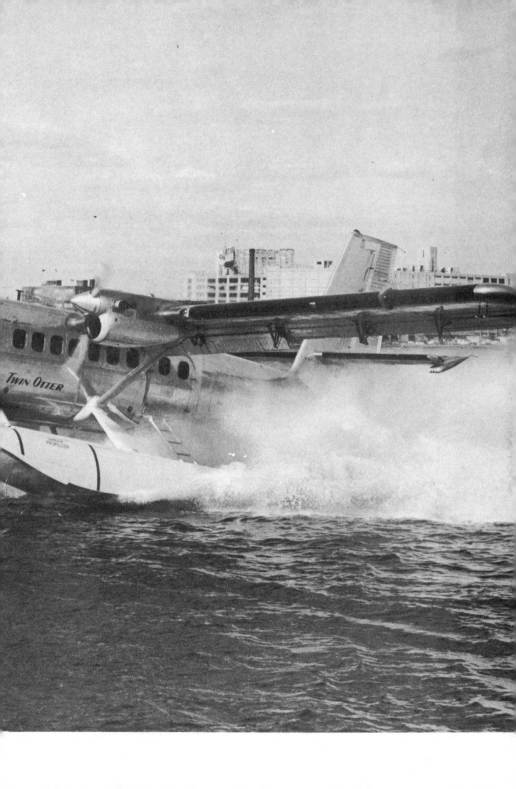

De Havilland Beaver float plane, popular in lake-dotted Canada

These three flying boats, the M-12, the PS-1 and the CL-214, useful aircraft as they are, however, may well be the last of a dying branch of aviation development.

There seems no major future for military flying boats, although Shin Meiwa naturally hope that the PS-1 is the first in the renaissance of the military seaplane. Even if this proves to be the case, there seems little likelihood of a major swing to water-based military aircraft. The most that can be envisaged is the development of a small number of aircraft for very specialised duties.

There seems to be no place either for the operation of large flying boats in the future civil aviation scene. This conclusion is reached in spite of several prophetic forecasts by flying boat protagonists regarding the increasing difficulties of building new land airports or of extending existing ones, due

Lake Buccaneer four-seat amphibian

to the scarcity of available land or to the vociferous protests of affected environmentalists.

One fundamental fact is that few major cities in the world are located near existing stretches of water suitable for large scale flying boat operations. Flying boat enthusiasts have often claimed that virtually any stretch of water of adequate length forms a natural and always ready-to-use runway. Unfortunately, this is rarely the case. Most of the large stretches of water near important cities are busy shipping lanes and in any case have to be continually swept clear of debris, just as concrete runways have to be.

Even where there are suitable areas of water, as at Toronto, Canada, and Cleveland, in the U.S., little or no thought was given to the possibility of introducing flying boat operations when new airports were required by these two major cities. In fact, on the other hand serious consideration has been given to the development of 'floating runways', from which landbased

155

airliners could operate. When plans were made in the 1960s for a third airport to serve London's growing needs, the site finally selected was at Maplin, on the Thames estuary, but the airport envisaged was to be built on land ironically largely reclaimed from the sea. The Maplin plan was eventually shelved. When the little island of Madeira needed to expand its air links with Europe, the harbour was not enlarged to accommodate more of the flying boats which had served it so well for many years, but a small and potentially dangerous runway for landplanes was built at enormous cost.

Although stretches of water do act as 'self-levelling' runways as one flying boat enthusiast proclaimed, an inherent disadvantage is the difficulty of determining the height above the surface, especially during the critical moments on the approach and before touchdown — and the extreme difficulty of providing the complex arrays of lights and other devices which have been developed to assist pilots to land safely on runways.

Perhaps the major factor against the large scale development and operation of civil flying boats, however, is the lack of the vast infrastructure of passenger and cargo access, accommodation and handling facilities required for contemporary mass air transportation, which has been developed over the past quarter of a century for landbased operations at phenomenal cost. This massive investment of capital is unlikely to be thrown away.

Neither are there suitable counterparts of the wide variety of specialised equipment such as tractors, ground power units, water servicing units, toilet servicing units, cargo container vehicles, engine slanting units, re-fuelling tankers and servicing platforms.

The development and provision of this infrastructure and equipment would be exceedingly expensive and would far outweigh any marginal economic advantages that might be offered by flying boats. To introduce them on environmental grounds alone would not be economically feasible.

As far as passengers are concerned, it is perhaps the stupendous growth of air travel brought about by the development of large 'jumbo' airliners, that has helped to make flying boats obsolete, by acting as a catalyst for the construction of airports and facilities all over the world. Although designed for mass transportation, many existing airports are at their wits end in attempting to cope with further growth. A water environment would, generally, compound the problem.

*   *   *

Early in this book the story was told of the world's first scheduled 'airline' flights operated by Benoist seaplanes of the St Petersburg —

Lake Buccaneer holiday camping site

Tampa Airboat Line in Florida. The review of flying boats ends with the story of what has been claimed to be the world's oldest airline and which has achieved this unique distinction despite the fact that throughout its life it has concentrated on floatplane and flying boat operations.

Known as Chalk's International Airline, after its founder 'Pappy' Chalk, it started operations from Miami, Florida, on 1st June 1919, six months after Prohibition became law. As the one and only pilot of his airline, 'Pappy' flew illegal bootleggers and lawful tax collectors alike, back and forth between Miami and Bimini in a three-seat Stinson *Voyager* fitted with floats. Sometimes a whisky-runner would make a particularly handsome 'rake-off', and would then spend some of it by chartering the Chalk aircraft for a trip up the Mississippi. In the early days Al Capone, the notorious ganster who lived on nearby Star Island, was a frequent user of the infant airline.

When Prohibition was repealed in 1933, 'Pappy' promoted the custom of big game fishermen and flew such personalities as Howard Hughes, Errol Flynn and Hemingway on charter flights to the Bahamas.

The little airline prospered during the 1930s and, enlarging into a fleet of floatplanes and amphibians, became the one which the 'fast set' of the day used to travel around their Bahamian playground. The area was a popular one for the location of adventure films and for many years the airline was busy flying movie people about.

The airline continued to prosper modestly, offering a simple 'no-frills' service of the kind which is only just being introduced by the big airline operators with their 'new' "sky-trains" and "shuttle" services. No food or

157

drinks are served on the Chalk flights. There are no stewardesses. There are no toilets. Cutting out cabin service and catering on the short routes saves both the airline and its passengers money and time.

The sixty years of Chalk operations has been over and across the notorious 'Burmuda Triangle', the area in which a number of ships and aircraft have disappered without trace. No harm due to 'unknown' causes, however, has ever befallen the Chalk aircraft. Throughout its life, Chalk's has always operated either flying boats, float planes or amphibians. In the early 1970s it acquired five Grumman Mallard amphibians, these being followed by the acquisition of Grumman Albatross amphibians.

However, both these aircraft are over 20 years old and it is a sad thought that there are no new comparable aircraft to which the airline can turn when they come to the end of their aeronautical lives. The age of the flying boat and sea plane has been short and glorious and if this last outpost is snuffed out, the Age will finally have ended.

*　　*　　*

Of relevant interest, however, is the report issued in late 1979 by a special committee set up by Japanese aerospace companies to investigate the commercial applications of flying boats. The report recommended serious studies on the use of flying boats in commercial service, as a possible solution to the difficulties in obtaining land for airports and solving related environmental problems.

Of even greater interest is the project announced late in 1979 by Shin Meiwa, manufacturer of the PS-1 and US-1 turboprop flying boats, for a 40-seat STOL jet amphibian. The proposed amphibian is of conventional layout with the exception of the high-set, wing-mounted turbofans. Such a civil aircraft is, of course, a more difficult proposition than the military PS-1 and US-1, but Shin Meiwa believe that it would be a practical solution for island studded countries such as Japan itself, and Indonesia and the Philippines. Evidence of their seriousness regarding the project, is the parallel study of the associated ground and water support equipment required, something often neglected in the past.

It is too soon to indicate whether the project will ever be built, but the business-like approach of Shin Meiwa towards the many problems is encouraging.

INDEX